A Primer for
Local
Historical
Societies

◆

D0792612

A Primer for Local Historical Societies

Laurence R. Pizer

Second Edition

*Revised and Expanded from the First Edition
by Dorothy Weyer Creigh*

American Association for State and Local History
Nashville, Tennessee

Published by the American Association for State and Local History, an international non-profit membership organization. For membership information, please contact Membership Services, (615) 255-2971.

95   94   93   92   91   5   4   3   2   1

Permission to use photographs by Anthony I. Baker (pp. 16, 26, 81, 83) courtesy of the Pilgrim Society, Plymouth, Massachusetts.

Permission to use all other photographs and illustrations courtesy of *The Soperton News*, J. Clayton Stephens, Jr., and the Treutlen County Historical Society, Soperton, Georgia.

Library of Congress Cataloging-in-Publication Data

Pizer, Laurence R., 1946–
    A primer for local historical societies / Laurence R. Pizer. —
2nd ed., rev. and expanded.
      p.   cm.
    Rev. ed. of: A primer for local historical societies / Dorothy
Weyer Creigh. c1976.
    Includes bibliographical references and index.
    ISBN 0-942063-12-0
    1. Historical societies—United States.   2. United States-
-History, Local—Societies, etc.   I. Creigh, Dorothy Weyer. Primer
for local historical societies.   II. Title.
E172.P58   1991
973'.06—dc20   91–14071
                                                       CIP

To

Dorothy Creigh

Her vision of "the possible" for local historical societies drove her
and all around her to great work.

Contents

———————◆———————

Preface
The Second Edition

◆

When a group of south central Nebraskans organized the Adams County Historical Society in 1966, its members followed a practice as old as the eighteenth century in gathering to organize the history of their area. Shortly after the founding, a native daughter, Dorothy Weyer Creigh, joined with them and suggested that they spearhead the writing of the centennial history of the county. She agreed to be the project director. The resulting work won an AASLH Award of Merit and the admiration of historians, in both Adams County and beyond.

Not content to return the gathered documentation to its previously disorganized state, Dorothy began a search for a "cataloguer" to work for six months to set up the collection. The first step was to find the necessary funds. With faith and drive, the society asked AASLH how to find an appropriate candidate, and it hired its first paid employee for a guaranteed six-month term and found him and his family a rental house with a one-year lease.

In gathering documentation for the centennial history, the society found itself in possession of hundreds of feet of 1920s movies of the locality. The group determined to develop a half-hour television program. Funding was difficult to find until an application to the National Endowment for the Humanities expanded the project to a series of television programs on the history of the Great Plains, based on the expanding collections of the society.

The society sent its employee, now called executive director, to AASLH seminars for training, it hired additional personnel, and it approached state funding agencies for money to expand its programming. It made a name for itself in its community and across the country.

The Adams County Historical Society set as its goal to be an example for historical societies, clearly recognizing that while the names and faces change, local history contains themes that all can appreciate. The excitement of local history comes from the changes in details, but each group can learn from the totality of experience.

This book will provide suggestions for societies to organize themselves for the benefit of local history. All of us know that financing is tight, but we also know that enthusiasm is contagious. When we work in local history, we become part of an important field. It is our obligation to learn how to do our work effectively.

It is a special honor for the Adams County Historical Society to have provided a member of its board of directors, Dorothy Weyer Creigh, as author of the first edition of this book and its first executive director, myself, as author of the second.

Laurence R. Pizer
Director, Pilgrim Society
Plymouth, Massachusetts

A Primer for
Local
Historical
Societies

◆

1

Before You Organize In the Beginning . . .

This book and your historical society must begin with planning. Before you can succeed, you must know what you are trying to accomplish.

Why do you want to have a historical society? What functions and purposes do you have in mind?

Do you see the society as a museum, housing collections of furniture, kitchen utensils, clothing, and artifacts of the past, showing this generation how another generation lived?

Or as a library, housing photographs, newspapers, documents, diaries and scrapbooks, manuscripts and tape recordings, providing research materials?

Or as a site-marking group, locating exact places where significant events took place, telling who lived, or fought, or invented and why that was important?

Or as the restoration of a fine old building or cluster of buildings, recreated to show precisely how another generation lived, with furniture, leaded windows, floor coverings, and auxiliary pieces in place?

Or as a publishing group, researching and printing stories about the past, distributing them to members and to the public?

Chances are you have a combination of purposes in mind when you begin. Decide what are the most urgent needs in your community for a historical society to fulfill, what are the inclinations and talents of the people who will be your members, and what are the financing possibilities of the group. You will be much stronger if you establish a list of priorities.

What is your scope?

Will the scope of your historical society be general history, preserving materials from all periods of the historic past, or will it be specific? Will you concentrate on a specific period to the exclusion of others?

Or will the scope be limited to a particular trade or profession? Will your society specialize in preserving material only about coal mining or sugar-beet growing or automobile production?

Will the scope be limited to a particular ethnic or racial group—a historical society for blacks, Chicanos, or Germans from Russia?

Most historical societies, particularly ones organized in and by a community rather than by a specialized group, are general in scope, tending to focus on all of the historic past in a geographic area—the history of Plymouth County or Brockton. They may have more material on one period than another—there may be more furniture from the Victorian era than the 1920s—but most local historical societies tend to be all-inclusive historically, preserving materials from all periods.

The definition of scope is vital. No organization can collect everything effectively, so knowing what to gather and what to leave uncollected will determine how efficient your organization will be. If an important item inappropriate to your collection is offered to you, you can turn to another organization, which can provide better care for the object. Everything you collect requires work on your part—to protect it, to catalogue it, to preserve it—so you must know what your area of interest is.

If yours is an all-inclusive society, do not overlook the fact that what happens today is part of history. The old days are glamorous and exciting, simply because they are alien. We can remember what happened yesterday. But last year's high-school annual will be a historical document in another twenty or fifty years.

Some communities already may have organized museums, but do not have historical societies, or vice versa. The new one can be organized as an adjunct to the already established institution or may be a completely separate entity. The new historical society can work cooperatively with other existing agencies, their common interests and even space requirements being compatible. A case in point is a public library, which frequently has the beginnings of a historical collection. The patrons of the library are often history buffs, and conversely, people who enjoy history are usually great users of library facilities.

There is no single avenue better than all others. Determine what you want to accomplish through a historical society, what is already in existence in the community, and what is the best organizational form for you. Do not duplicate efforts nor set up a competing organization. History is for harmony. The public may withdraw its support if it perceives unnecessary competition.

Who are your members?

Will your membership be open to everyone who wants to join, no matter where they were born or grew up? Will it be limited, open only to old-timers or first families?

If your membership is exclusive, you will necessarily limit the size of the organization and probably its effectiveness. The sheer quantity of work you will need to accomplish is staggering, and the number of willing workers is an important factor in your success.

Some communities have discovered that, even more than some old-timers, newcomers are interested in the history at the area because they want to know what happened before they came. Through the aegis of the Welcome Wagon or similar enterprise, historical societies in some communities provide newcomers with packets, including a brief history of the town, maps of historic sites in the area, sample copies of the societies' publications, and information about membershp. Newcomers

Hold a reception to let the community know that a historical society is going to be organized.

Be sure to set the mood for your event—history and music go well together.

will be enticed to join your society if they believe it is the place to meet the established members of the community. In most instances, a mix of new and old will prove successful for the organization.

How do you finance the society?

For what purposes will the society need money? You will quickly find that you require both large donations for capital one-time expenses and ongoing income for general operating expenses.

Before you organize, you should divide your treasury by defining how money will be spent. What will happen to a gift made to your organization? Why should someone buy a membership in the society? For what purposes and how effectively will be money be spent?

Where do you get help?

The community of historical agencies stands ready to welcome an energetic newcomer to the fold. Your state historical society (a list of addresses is given in Appendix A) will be delighted that you will represent a locality and provide direct representation to your population. The American Association for State and Local History (172 Second

Avenue North, Suite 202, Nashville, Tennessee 37201) has books and leaflets available on a wide variety of subjects. The arts and humanities agencies in all states are open to inquiries from new societies.

How do you begin?

As soon as you are ready to start, fix a date and time and place for a meeting. Use all available means of publicity to get the word out that a historical society is to be organized. Send well-written articles to the newspapers, dailies, weeklies, and shoppers' guides. Ask the state historical society to announce the meeting in its newsletter. Make announcements in history classes and meetings of community organizations (like the Rotary), church groups, and unions. Post notices on bulletin boards at supermarkets and launderettes. Let the community know that it is welcome and needed.

If possible, you might coordinate the organization of the society with an event, like the centennial of the community or the dedication of a major facility or the commemoration of a historic undertaking.

2

♦

Organizing

The nucleus group that is organizing your historical society should draft a constitution and simple bylaws, outlining the purposes of the group, lists of officers and trustees, their duties and tenure, and the time of an annual meeting. As with all legal documents, the simpler the better. If your bylaws are too restrictive, they will have to be changed often. At the same time, they should design an organization in which the locus of authority for action and for finance is clearly defined. Your state historical society may have sample bylaws for you and suggestions for what will work.

It is to your advantage to interest a good lawyer and a good accountant in your organization. Their advice at early stages will get you off to a good start.

Try to enlist the help of people who have energy, enthusiasm, imagination, and expertise in specialized fields; your organization will be dependent on volunteer workers, and you need as many people with expert knowledge as possible. Encourage the attendance of people you know will work and follow through on their promises to join the society.

It is true that you will need someone to pour tea at the tea party (and to provide the teapot), but you need even more people to wash teacups in the kitchen! Have as varied a group of historically minded members as you can find. Seek a broad spectrum in the community, people from many professions, economic levels, and social strata. Include all ages, too. Young people understand what is real and are the least hooked by unprovable legends. The historical society many be one of few places in the community where the young and the old come together in an appreciation of what each group has to contribute to the whole.

9

At the first meeting, elect officers and trustees. Have the slate fairly well settled before the meeting, but do not be inflexible. Someone intensely interested may show up at the first meeting. The trustees should be representative of the community, not an established clique.

Your two most important officers at first will be the president and the treasurer. The president represents the organization to the public, oversees all planning, appoints members to committees, and keeps track of the entire organization. The treasurer is in charge of financial matters. Your secretary is the clerk of the corporation and will be the legal signatory for government matters as well as the person keeping track of minutes.

The board of trustees or an executive committee of the board will plan all the activities of the organization; they are the policy-makers, responsible for decisions about long-range goals. They are entrusted with the general overall aims rather than with specific day-to-day events. They also hold general responsibility for the organization, seeing that sufficient funding is in place to support activities.

Before you are financially able to hire a staff, separate committees will be charged with the specific operating functions of the organization. What those functions are will depend on the purposes of the society. The committees should be defined so that they will have enough work to keep them occupied without exhausting them. Some committees should be defined in the bylaws, and others should be ad hoc, appointed by the president for one-time purposes.

Because it is likely that at first you will not have a permanent location for your historical society or at least one that will be manned all the time, it is wise to rent a post office box for continuity of mailing address. As you change officers through the years, the number of the box remains the same.

The treasurer will establish a bank account to make all the financial transactions of the society by check. The bylaws should establish procedures for approval of bills. In general, it is wise for at least two individuals to be involved, one to approve bills and another to pay them, following approval of the budget by the trustees.

A very early priority is incorporation as a nonprofit institution so that gifts can be deducted on donors' income tax returns. Following incorporation by your state, seek a letter of determination from the Internal Revenue Service, which certifies your tax-exempt status. In most instances, your tax exemption will fall under Section 501(c)3 of the IRS code.

Another early task is the development of a distinctive logo or print-

Develop a distinctive logo for stationery and certificates. This group uses a pine tree to symbolize their region's chief natural resource.

ing style for the organization to appear on membership bills, gift certificates, gift acknowledgments, stationery, and envelopes.

The next step is the presentation of the first program. Programming is the reason for your existence, and it is what will attract a wider public. The first programs need not be complicated. A lecture by a local, well-respected speaker on a topic central to your organization's mission will set the tone. The topic should be colorful, thought-provoking, specific, and, most of all, historical. It should be something the audience can relate to, from either personal experience or lore passed down to them from other generations. It should excite thought and memories and spark their imaginations.

Your goal will be the preservation and organization of the history of your subject: tape record the lecture or get a written copy. Also use the public gathering to make a short presentation on what the organization will seek to accomplish and what the audience can do about it.

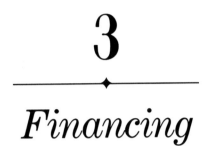

3

Financing

Whatever your type of organization, there are going to be expenses involved. Whether the organization is run by volunteers or professionals, the public is receiving benefits from your existence. Someone is going to have to pay for the organization. Do not be ashamed to ask those who can afford to pay to show their support financially.

Memberships

Memberships represent one of the first souces of income for many organizations. It is wise to determine from the start a financial reason for individuals to join. Do you see membership as a donation to the cause, or do members receive benefits related to the amount they pay?

Memberships should cover at the very least the expenses associated with programs free to members. If you have a newsletter, determine the costs for all of the issues and the postage to send them out. If you can, see that membership funds support not only the newsletter but additional activities as well.

One plan for membership provides an annual fee for individuals, another for families, and a life membership charge. A family membership recognizes that most privileges are the same whether or not a husband and wife both join or just one does. Therefore, the cost should be just a bit higher than an individual membership.

A typical range for memberships is $15 or $20 for an individual, $5 or $10 more for a family, and $200 or $300 for a life membership. Some organizations offer a special rate for life memberships for a couple taken out at the same time with the same rationale as family annual membership.

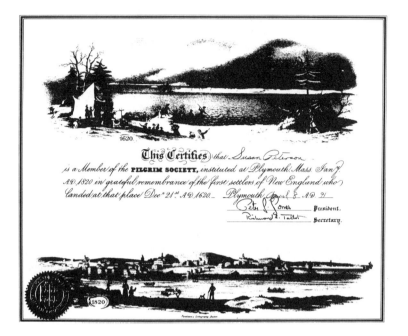

Make your members feel they are an important part of the organization. A distinctive membership certificate of the Pilgrim Society features scenes of Plymouth, Massachusetts, in 1620 and in 1820 (Pendleton's Lithography, Boston) to illustrate the founding of the organization.

For private groups, membership is both a source of income and ownership of the organization. If you offer complimentary memberships, be sure to state what privileges are connected with them, specifically whether or not the complimentary members have voting privileges. There might come a time when the election of the president of a divided organization could hinge on a few votes.

You must understand both the tax structure of the country and the spending habits of the community before you can decide what to charge for membership. By and large the Internal Revenue Service states that if a payer receives benefits for money, that money cannot be considered a donation and is not tax deductible. Therefore, if you develop a membership structure that provides sliding benefits based on the amount given, the generous person who is more interested in providing you with funds than he or she is in special services will be unneccesarily robbed of a legitimate deduction. If your community follows the practice of donation to causes it supports, you might wish to develop classifications of donations rather than classifications of membership.

If you decide to provide life memberships, you must treat the funds raised as capital rather than as annual operating income. Most organizations provide their members with free admission or publications or discounts, so there must be a continuing source of funds to provide that. There is nothing wrong with investing the life membership payments and using the proceeds for operating expenses. Life memberships should be set high enough to generate sufficient income, at least ten to fifteen times the annual rates.

If you have a scheme in which individuals fall into brackets like benefactor, patron, and sustaining member, you will need a ruling from the Internal Revenue Service to determine that amounts over the basic rate are tax deductible as a contribution. If you provide additional services to more expensive memberships, the ruling becomes more complicated.

Like most finanical areas of your operations, memberships will have to be sold. A letter to the community will bring in some people, but personal solicitation will accomplish far more. At renewal time, the first step should be a reminder letter, but each year the work of a committee will lead to a larger membership.

If you have a sliding scale, you will need to sell the importance of higher categories. You should not be reluctant about promoting the importance of providing growing amounts. Most individuals are accustomed to modern fund-raising techniques. On your level, you will have to promote your organization actively.

City or county support

Many historical societies receive mill levies or outright grants from city or county boards. Some states have passed legislation making it possible for cities or counties to assess property taxes for the support of local historical societies.

If you want to appear before the city council or county commissioners to ask for financial support, plan your performance in some detail in advance. Get in touch with the leaders of the board well ahead of time to discuss with them your chances of getting support; there is no point in appearing before them and being turned down if there was no reasonable expectation of success. Find out the best time for your appearance; the meeting considering a major tax increase is not a good opportunity.

Prepare a succinct, carefully worded paper listing why you need money, what your programs are, and why it would be advantageous to the county for you to receive the funds. When you are seeking public funds, it is essential that you explain that what you are doing will serve the entire public; you must persuade the council that an active historical society will stimulate pride in the community and perhaps draw tourists to spend money.

It would be best to provide this material to the board in writing before the meeting so the members can consider it at their leisure. When you appear before the board, be prepared to answer questions and to be brief. If you expect to run into some opposition from anti-tax groups, have some sympathetic taxpayers in the audience. They can add weight and authority to your cause.

The directors of one historical society spent several weeks preparing for their appreance before a county board, even dividing up answers to possible questions. To their astonishment and delight, their request was granted in sixty seconds with a single question, "Why didn't you come sooner?"

Entrance fees

Most museums must charge for admission, and the public in the United States has come to expect such fees. A judgment on the appropriate entrance fee depends on what similar attractions in the area charge and what will be seen as reasonable by potential visitors.

Be certain that you determine whose money you expect to collect. If the local populace forms your basic audience and if you are tax-supported, you might not want to charge for admission. If you never expect to draw well outside the local populace, an admission charge might not be advisable. On the other hand, everyone who receives services from you should pay for them, so you might devise a suggested payment for outside visitors and expect that most of them will support you.

A donation box near the entrance and exit can provide funds, especially if your admission fee is modest. The real question is one of effectiveness. What combination of fees will provide the greatest level of support over the longest period?

Donations

In the United States, people are accustomed to the idea of supporting institutions through contributions. You need to gain your share.

The first step lies in establishing programs that show your society is worthy of support. A corollary to this is publicizing your efforts so that the public knows about your work.

The second step is turning your potential support into cash. For this you will need a large corps of volunteers willing to ask for money. Few people enjoy pleading for support, but the work is vital to the success of most organizations.

A campaign for individual support and a separate effort for corporate support will stand you in good stead. Explain to potential donors what their gifts will support. Get the right members of your board to make the plea to key donors. It is absolutely true that many people will give in the hope that those making the request will return the favor for another charitable cause.

Other money-raising projects

There are as many money-raising projects as there are people to imagine them. The real issue is how the projects represent your organization. The public needs to support you, but it also needs to separate you in its mind from the church or charity in which it also is interested. Whenever you can, you should attach something historical to your fund raising.

One historical society raised several thousand dollars holding a fashion show, but it made sure that most of the fashions were historical. A carnival or fair will draw attention and money, and booths reminiscent of the past will bring a special flair. A lecture series during the summer could be sponsored by many types of groups, but a Chautauqua suggests a historical society.

Your fund-raising projects should contribute in an important way to your organization's coffers even after you deduct the time that could have been spent elsewhere. Different projects are appropriate during different stages of an organization's existence.

A newly formed county historical society planned several projects to raise funds during its early years. Guided tours of the county, sales of food at farm auctions, and publication of county maps all brought in funds that put the group on a solid footing and simultaneously convinced the public of the energy of the group.

Years later, the group had developed a large list of programs with an energetic and varied funding effort. When the budget committee bemoaned the difficulty of balancing the budget, one long-time trustee suggested a food auction, which had always cleared dozens of dollars. It was necessary to remind the member that the annual budget had risen from a few hundred dollars to tens of thouands. Twelve donors to the publication program were giving several hundred dollars per month to show their name off in the masthead of the journal. Their impression of being in league with food at farm auctions would be negative. Anything with a historical connection or anything that suggested culture brought up no such questions, since the activity was directly related to the mission of the historical society or suggested an allied enterprise.

State and federal grants for specific projects

Grants have a particular mystique for new societies. The uninitiated assume that they are tainted somehow because they are government money, that there is a secret to securing them, or that they are reserved for only the fanciest of organizations. None of that is true, but knowledge about the granting process is valuable to improve one's changes of receiving such support.

Grants represent programs the government wishes to see developed. They are cooperative ventures between the government, which provides at least some of the funding, and a sponsoring organization, which provides the inspiration and the manpower. If a society understands that grants are not gifts, but joint efforts, it will have gone a long way toward figuring out how to approach them.

Think of the staff of the granting agency as people dedicated to seeing that their money is spent as effectively as possible toward the stated ends of the agency. Therefore, staffs of granting agencies neither hoard the funds, since that would produce no programming, nor do they throw funds around, since that would be ineffective. Their work is to find the right organization and the right program to spend their money and bring enlightenment to the public.

Their staffs can work most effectively if they deal with you directly. Do not waste their time, but communicate with them personally whenever you have a legitimate question. Given a comparatively small number of historical organizations, granting agencies almost always would rather talk to you about a project than have it fail or be less strong than it might be.

Granting agencies seek as broad a group of grantees as possible. In one situation a state humanities council asked a rather young historical society to write a letter to other historical societies explaining how easy it was to work with the council. The historical society had believed that it was specially blessed by the money from the humanities council, and the humanities council was delighted by the quality of the historical society.

Many granting agencies change their emphasis with some frequency, even annually. They might concentrate on ethnic groups one year and on occupations the next, depending on political considerations and public needs. It is important to remain aware of guidelines and specific interests.

It is your obligation to learn about grant opportunities. When you are seeking funding for projects, those considering making a donation will want to know how intelligently you pursue reasonable opportunities for money. They expect you to know as much as possible about grant programs.

National agencies

The National Endowment for the Arts and the National Endowment for the Humanities are the two major granting agencies for specific projects of historical societies. While they state no official preference for large organizations over small, their responsibility nationally leads them, for the most part, toward funding projects with wide scope. That, in many cases, leads them toward funding large organizations.

Small historical societies are not excluded though. One small historical society found outstanding early local motion pictures and asked the National Endowment for the Humanities to fund a local television program. NEH responded by suggesting the possibility of a series on the entire region. The endowment was pleased to provide funds to a new organization, and the historical society was willing to enlarge the scope of its work.

The Institute of Museum Services limits its scope to museums, but its operating support reaches museums of all sizes. Its annual competition for funding pits small groups against small and large against large, looking for quality rather than size. It also provides conservation grants and funds for institutional assessments.

Other national agencies have funds for designated purposes, and historical societies are eligible to apply. Employment programs, archaeological progams, science programs, and more emanate from many federal agencies. It is the job of the historical society to uncover them.

State agencies

Both the arts and humanities endowments grant money to each state for regranting by state-based agencies. The names vary, but each state has an arts council and a humanities agency to provide funding for locally oriented programs. While these grants tend to be smaller than federal grants, they are far more widespread and much more likely to come your way.

Someone in your organization should meet with appropriate staff of each of these agencies to determine how their money and your ideas can match. They will be more impressed with you if they can associate a face with inquiries.

Some grant moneys are almost embarrassingly easy to gather. Pressure from the arts community forced at least one state with a lottery to designate some funds for local distribution for arts projects. A town agency might need to grant $5,000 twice a year, and you should make your organization available to asist them.

Wherever you are applying for money, here are a few points that will assist you:

- Be honest and forthright. You are establishing a long-term relationship with an agency.
- Plan carefully. Most granting agencies are understaffed, and, while they are willing to work with you, they do not want to waste time.
- Do your homework. Know what the agency is looking for and provide it, if it is in your interest. It is useful to build your reputation for wisdom and success with an agency. Its staff will look upon future applications with a positive expectation.

Foundations

There are hundred of thousands of foundations in the United States, listed in several guides, since they are required by the Internal Revenue Service to reveal their interests and figures. A few are well known; most are small and out of reach.

The guidelines for foundations are similar to those for government agencies. Prepare by learning about the interests of foundation. Asking a family foundation for funds, when the purpose of the foundation is to provide a college eduation for the children of the founder, wastes everyone's time. In many instances, the trustees of a small foundation are bankers or trust officers who also work with larger ones. You do not want them to think of you as ineffective and careless.

The greatest likelihood of success will lie with medium-sized foundations in your area with stated interests in funding specific types of projects that meet your needs. Learn about the application process and follow the advice of the trust officers.

Audits

As soon as possible, arrange for an audit by a certified public accounting firm. In your early years, some accountants will perform the work as a public service, but it is important that the work be done. Not only will the accountant require proper procedures by your group, but the audit will legitimate you in the eyes of many outside agencies. Finances are one means of communicating your priorities to the rest of the world. An audited report does that in a clear manner.

Publicity

To carry out your work effectively, you will need the help of all available publicity. The public needs to know what you are doing in order to appreciate your work and to join with you in accomplishing it.

How to work with the news media

Most newspaper staffs as well as other news media rely heavily on prepared news releases. They are far more likely to run stories on your society if you provide ready-to-use material than if you ask for a reporter to cover an event. If you do not have a skilled newspaper reporter among your members, you will have to assign someone to learn the basics of reporting and newswriting.

When you have a story about some forthcoming event, write about it in acceptable newspaper style, telling the most important facts first and including the basic five W's plus the H—who, what, where, when, why, and how—in the first paragraph. Be accurate and spell all the names correctly. The story should be typed, double spaced, with a large margin at the top and adequate margins at each side. Always provide the name and telephone number of the person who wrote the story so that the newspaper staff can follow up the story and confirm the information.

Be sure you know the deadlines for the local newspaper and for the local radio and television stations. If you want the story to run in a particular issue of the newspaper or on local radio or television on a particular day, have the story in the office well ahead of the deadline. Many newspapers will be more likely to give your story good space if you do not specify a particular day for an advance story, but indicate

Displaying a recently discovered photo of the man for whom the town was named at a local bank created favorable publicity for the historical society.

that you want it to run some time prior to a given date. (Wednesday is grocery ad day for many daily newspapers, for instance, and there is more news space available in those larger issues.)

Many weekly newspapers are printed at a central printing shop and have deadlines several days in advance; for Thursday newspapers, for instance, the deadline for your type of copy usually is Monday.

Be aware of specific columns in which you can have reminders: social calendars or something similar appear in most papers. Use all the news space you possibly can to tell about your planned activities.

Many local or regional radio or television stations have community calendars that list events of the day. Write your paragraph convincingly—you need to sell your meeting—and be sure to list the who, what, when, and where. Send the story to the Community Calendar, or whatever it may be called, with a notation of which day or days you wish it to be read.

Local stations often have daytime community service interviews that allow you time to interpret the purposes of your historical society. It might be possible for you to set up a schedule of appearances every three months or at regular intervals, at least, with different individuals from the group appearing each time to explain different functions or activities.

Study your own situation carefully. What are the means by which people in your community learn about events? What columns do they read, what local television and radio news programs are most likely to carry your news?

After each meeting at which officers are elected, or volunteers given achievement pins, or some other newsworthy event, write the story and get it to the media immediately for their use. After an event has happened, the story must be in the newsroom as soon as possible—it is no longer news if you wait.

If you have had a particularly stimulating address, either write if up in precis form, quoting directly the most salient points, or send a copy of the speech, with the most interesting sentences underlined, to the newspaper office, along with a paragraph telling what the event was, where and when it was held, who the speaker was, and how many people attended. Make it easy for the local news media to use your material.

If you have a particularly significant story you think is of statewide importance, suggest to the local news editor that he or she put it on the Associated Press or United Press International wire. If the editor does not concur, do not argue—you may hurt your chances of future coverage.

When you have a story you think the newspaper or local television station would like to use with pictures, telephone the news editor well in advance so that a photographer and reporter can be scheduled to cover the event. Describe the happening and why you think it is worth pictorial coverage, and let the editor make the decision. If the editor decides not to send a photographer, do not wheedle or threaten. Although there may be some cost involved, you might consider producing and providing your own photography.

Establish a good rapport with the local editors of the news media. If you display a professionalism about your work with them, they will respect you and will cooperate with you. If you can get a reporter assigned to do an interpretive story at the founding of the society, you will have a supporter and interpreter on your side. If you cannot, be as helpful as you can to any member of the press with whom you work.

The more you understand about the working methods of the media, the easier it will be to persuade them to cover your events. *News* to them means something new. The most wonderful artifact in the state is worth one story unless you find a new angle for a second.

Alert the media in advance when a photo-worthy opportunity will occur.

How to use other sources

There are other means of publicity, too: posters displayed in store windows, especially grocery stores, and bulletin boards in shopping centers and launderettes; announcements in history classes and at club meetings of all kinds in the community; signboards on banks or other institutions in town. If you meet in a building belonging to a particular group—a church, a women's club, a grange hall—be sure its members know about you.

If you are having a membership drive or a significant event far enough in the future that exact timing of publicity is not essential, you can print brochures to be included in billings that the telephone company, the utility company, the bank, or department stores mail out. You and your volunteers may have to help stuff the envelopes, but those mailing are a good way of reaching many people. If you make arrangements in advance, grocery stores will often stuff printed sheets in bags at the checkout stand.

Carefully study the means by which people in your community learn about what is going on. If it is a party-line telephone, use that; if it is some other means, use that. Saturate your community with information about your historical society.

5

---◆---

Beginning Projects for Limited Budgets

The gathering and preservation of artifacts and manuscripts with their data and the interpretation and dissemination of such information are the primary purposes of historical societies.

To accumulate, preserve, interpret, and disseminate that history, you must make the community aware of it: aware, interested, proud, and involved with you in it. In its work a historical society can bring unity and harmony to a community, attracting the talents and energies of widely diverse groups and individuals, working together in a common cause.

However, if yours is like most historical societies, you will be long on ideas, imagination, and enthusiasm and short on cash. Here are some suggestions for beginning projects. They are simple and involve little financial outlay but considerable hard work and attention to detail. They serve the dual function of gathering and preserving history and of getting the community as a whole interested in the history of the area.

Meetings with speakers

A good beginning project is a series of meetings at regularly scheduled times, perhaps once a month, at which speakers deliver well-researched, detailed papers on specific subjects of local interest. The time should be limited to about thirty minutes per paper with no more than two papers per meeting. The speakers should indicate in their manuscripts the sources of their information, although they should not read those citations aloud as they present their papers.

The subjects should be strictly limited in scope. Ethnic culture programs provide ready-made topics. Why did the Bohemians or Swedes or whoever settle in the community, leave their homeland, and when? Why did they come to this particular area? Did they come as family groups, as individuals, or as whole colonies? What did they do for a living when they first came here? What have been their contributions to the community? What was their life like in the old country? There may be ethnic clubs or churches right in the area that would like to participate or help research the topic. There could be enough material for a number of programs.

Perhaps someone in the community has old letters or diaries for source material; interviews with old-timers and the scanning of old newspapers might turn up more. Perhaps some local genealogist could fill in some details for you. For a Great Plains community, a set of letters from a lawyer present at the founding of a community sent to his sweetheart back home were wonderfully revealing and poignant. The addition of a small bit of research filled in details of their later lives.

One local group engendered so much enthusiasm with its ethnic culture programs that afterward some of the participants organized a society of Germans from Russia, and others, a French-Canadian historical club, working closely with the historical society. In future years, the offshoot clubs will be able to provide programs themselves for the parent organization.

Other subjects could relate to specific industries. For instance, if yours is a manufacturing area, find out what attracted the first industries to the region and when, what the first ones were, and how the various industries have changed through the years. You will probably discover that you have unearthed material that the companies themselves do not know about. You could have a program on industries that no longer exist. You might have a whole series of programs, one on each specific industry.

If yours is a tobacco producing area, how about a program on the history of tobacco growing? Why did the early farmers decide to grow tobacco and when? What have been the different varieties grown through the years? How have production methods changed? Who have been some of the influential planters? What have been some of the problems? The more detail you can give, the more colorful you can make your presentations and the more interest listeners will show.

Think about changes. If an industry was there and now is not, there must be a reason.

One prairie historical society sponsored a lecture by a collector of barbed wire, with an intriguing study on the different kinds of barbed wire used by the early pioneers of the area. A western historical society asked a gun collector to speak on "Guns that Won the West," and a group of goggle-eyed little boys sat in the front row listening to every word.

The topics are endless. You can think of dozens—circuses of the past, the old ice house, bootlegging, intriguing murder cases or bank robberies, livery barns and horse races, crystal-set radios, the old red-light district; just ask yourself what you would like to know about your community.

The programs can be given by knowledgeable members of your own society, representatives from collectors' or hobby clubs, out-of-towners, or by anyone. Who gives the presentations is less important than the quality of the work that went into preparing and presenting them.

Be sure to save copies of the speeches for your permanent files. Tape record them too, after you have received permission from the speakers.

That is a passive sort of program in that only a few people do the work and the rest are spectators. As you build up the confidence and techniques, you can start planning some projects that call for more member participation.

Locating historical information

Since the accumulation of data is one of the primary purposes of your historical society, searching out that information provides a good project on which to concentrate in the early years of the organization. What material has already been published about your area? Where are copies located? And what is in them? You will want to prepare a list of what material is available and where it is: bibliographies and indexes.

Bibliographies

A bibliography is a list of books about a given subject. Even though you yourself may not have copies of those books, to know that they exist, what is in them, and where they are located is most useful.

In the late 1800s, many regional histories were published by commercial printing establishments, most of which financed their books by selling space in them for biographical or business information. Was a history of your community published? In the early 1900s, there was another rash of commercially printed local histories.

Even in recent years, enterprising people produced church histories on commission, providing only the depth for which the churches were willing to pay. Can you find those for your county?

What state histories include your locality? What pamphlets have been published—by railroads, by the local Chamber of Commerce? What school histories have been written?

A good starting point for finding local historical information is your state historical library. Spend time there, talking to the librarian and going through the card catalogue to find out what material that particular library lists in its files.

Privately owned collections make interesting displays for society meetings and will boost attendance.

Check the books themselves to see what is in them of particular significance to your society. Make lists, including the name of the book, author, publisher, date, and what is of interest to your group.

If you are, for example, the Fairfield, Nebraska, Historical Society, you may find a volume published in 1890 with material about Fairfield. Your entry would look like this:

_____ (No author listed), Biographical and Historical Memoirs of Adams, Clay, Webster, and Nuckolls Counties of Nebraska (Chicago: The Goodspeed Publishing Company, 1890). Clay County, Chapter XIX, pp. 341-363. Population, Elevations, Area, Rivers and Streams, Physical Formations, Grasshopper Plagues, Effect of Same, Storms and Blizzards. Chapter XX, Fairfield Journals and Periodicals, pp. 365-366; G.A.R. and Militia Lists, Fairfield, pp. 369-370. Chapter XXIV, pp. 387-530. Fairfield, Preemption of Town Sites, Original Buildings, Mayors, Commercial Interests, Fires, Water System, Education and Religious Matters, Secret and Benevolent Organizations, General History.

You would go through all the other pertinent books in the state historical library to see what other references are made to Fairfield and would make similar listings, in each case indicating that a copy of the book is located in the Nebraska State Historical Society library.

Check all sorts of magazines, too, using the Readers' Guide and any other appropriate reference works. The state historical quarterly, the state department of commerce or tourism or highway publications, or corporate magazines may have had stories in them about Fairfield. What material is in them, what are the dates and volume numbers of the magazine, and where are they located? Someday, you will have the originals in your library. In the meantime, the information composes your bibliography.

Indexes

At some time you should go back over that same material to make more detailed lists, according to subject matter, indexing your material. From the Goodspeed volume of 1890, for instance, you would list, "Newspaper, Fairfield, _____ (No author listed), Biographical and Historical Memoirs of Adams, Clay, Webster, and Nuckolls Counties of Nebraska, pp. 365-366." Under the newspaper listing, you would enter any other references from other books to newspapers in Fairfield. Whenever anyone wanted to find information about early newspapers in Fairfield, the catalogue index card, "Newspapers," would list the books, the page numbers, and locations of each book that refers to newspapers.

Indexing information is a time-consuming project, which will require the talents of many members of your group, but it is a worthwhile undertaking.

Members of your own historical society may have historical volumes of their own. Ask them to make similar listings from their own books, indicating what material is in them and where the books are located—entries for both your bibliographical listing and your index. When you are doing research on a specific subject, you will be able to tell quickly what material is available and where to find it.

If churches or schools in your area have celebrated anniversaries, perhaps they published pamphlets or booklets. Who has them? What is in them? Try to locate them and make listings of their contents.

Who in your community keeps scrapbooks, and what is in them of historical interest? You can do the same sort of indexing and listing for them as for books. Where are old school annuals located?

Local newspapers are probably the best single source of all. Your newspaper office may contain a morgue of clippings about various subjects. If it is a small newspaper office, perhaps the editor will let you make listings of subjects, particularly if the clippings go back into the past, so that you will know what material is there. Offer the editor help in organizing or maintaining the morgue, if need be. Such service will help both your institutions.

Where are the old newspapers of your community kept? You will not start out making an index of stories in them—perhaps sometime—but at least have an indication in your files of where they are located and the exact dates of the issues.

When you have located them, if they are not on microfilm, consider helping to get them on film. The state historical society or state library commission may have funds available for that purpose. Check with them. The editor of the local newspaper may be more amenable to letting papers out of the building for filming if the suggestion comes from local people, especially if you can explain to the editor that once the newspapers are on film, located somewhere else, the newspaper staff will not have to tolerate people coming to the office to look up old stories. In fact, the editor may even help you with the donation of a microfilm reader.

Consider the creation of an index as detective work. You may start out using a shoe box, but your depository will grow eventually into a bank of card drawers.

Collecting historical material

Another project you will want to begin soon is the collecting of all kinds of historical materials: manuscripts, books, records, photographs, and other source material. Use all kinds of procedures to get the word out that you are interested in collecting such material. Tell your members to talk to their friends—word-of-mouth is an effective means of publicizing your needs. Another effective means is the local newspaper. Have a reporter write a clever feature story connecting the rites of spring with your need for old photographs, books, and other historical material. Perhaps you could arrange an interview on the local radio station to talk about the project. Use whatever means you have at hand to publicize the fact that you are looking for source materials for a historical library.

If you know that a family in the community is about to move from its home, ask the family not to throw out any pictures or papers until you have had a chance to look them over. The garbage dumps of this country contain a sickening amount of history, particularly old photographs the owners did not want to keep.

What will you want to save? Anything that pertains to the history of your area: letters describing specific events or giving details of the past; manuscripts of speeches made about the town; term papers that students have written about the community; academic dissertations—anything that adds specific historical knowledge. If the manuscripts are copyrighted, be sure they are so marked so that you will know how to handle literary rights if you ever wish to publish information from them.

One family recently found a little notebook in which an ancestor, at the age of eleven, had begun to list the various game birds he saw every day in the 1880s. The notebook is now tremendously valuable, both for the historical society and for the state game commission, for it tells exactly what kinds of birds and other game were in the area then, on what days, and in what approximate quantities. The notebook is not the scientific listing of an ornithologist, but in the absence of other records, the jottings of an eleven-year-old boy are important.

Old letters, journals, and diaries are significant, especially if they are clear, vivid accounts of what was taking place when they were written. Scrapbooks can be important if they include photographs, clippings, and memorabilia—ticket stubs, programs, menus, and the like—carefully labeled as to dates and events, with each picture carefully identified.

Books, of course, you will want—all kinds that tell about your community. From your bibliographical lists, you will know something about what books have been published, but be on the lookout constantly for others. You will want to collect commemorative booklets of churches, schools, and businesses; Chamber of Commerce brochures; school annuals; pamphlets issued at the time of dedication of a hospital or other public building giving architectural and background data—any books that will add to your knowledge of the community.

You do not want all books. A pretty binding around information not germane to your subject is a waste of shelf space. You will be offered more Bibles than you thought possible. Accept only those with marginal notes of serious importance to your subject even if the potential donors threaten to destroy them unless you accept them.

You will want photographs, with negatives, if you can find them. Be sure that each photograph is carefully labeled when you accept it: what occasion is pictured, who the people are—their exact names, not "Mother" or "Aunt Bertha"—where and when the picture was taken—the exact date if possible.

Be careful in labeling or identifying pictures that you do not mar them. You obviously will never mark on the face of the photograph. Treat the back carefully so that the impression of any writing does not show through. You might assign a file number, written in an inconspicuous place on the back of the photograph, and then provide detailed identifying information in your card catalogue.

If your local newspaper tosses out prints or pictures after they have been published, ask if you can have them for your files. Be certain to find out if the newspaper's developing process provides lasting images to avoid wasting time. After high school or other annuals have been printed, ask if you can have the photographs for your files. Those pasteups usually lie around for a year or so and are then thrown out, destroying good sources of pictorial history.

Establish a good rapport with the local newspaper and commercial photographers from your community to make arrangements with them for lists of their negatives. Ten years from now, if you need a picture of a particular building dedication, for instance, you will know where to locate the negative. If you establish a friendly relationship with commercial photographers in the area, you can be of service to them when they clean out their files of negatives. You can claim some for historical purposes, sorting and filing them for your society. The photographer can claim a legitimate tax deduction for a donation to a charitable institution. Negatives should be filed, one to an envelope, with names, occasion, location, and date carefully noted on the envelopes or with identifying numbers leading to such data arranged elsewhere. If you can afford it, consider having a copy negative made when someone lends you a print that you wish you had in the collection.

You will also want to acquire movies of your community. In your area, there surely have been amateur photographers who have shot movies through the years. Locate them and acquire those you can; make listings of those you cannot obtain so that when you have sufficient funds, you can duplicate them. Movies are a startling source of social history. Even though much of the footage may seem to be simply children's birthday parties and Christmas celebrations, you can find invaluable glimpses of the times in the rest.

With the improvement in technology in videotaping, consider having brittle movies transferred to videotape. It might well be a cheaper means of saving the images.

If your community has a local television station, consider obtaining tapes of its local newscasts for your files. The tapes take a great deal of storage space but are significant sources of historical material.

Documentary records are primary source materials and should be preserved, using appropriate archival retention standards. That is to say that you should avoid saving duplicate material of easily accessible records. Keep your eyes peeled for school and church records, business files, and organizational records. You may well be the only institution saving them.

Governmental records usually fall under the jurisdiction of the secretary of state or the state archivist. Your job is to make sure that they are accessible to your constituency.

Churches and schools disband or unite with others, and their original records get lost in the shuffle. They are valuable historical source material. If you know the whereabouts of any old records now, acquire them. Frequently, they are in the attic of the last secretary. If you hear of any churches or schools that are about to change status, ask for all record books for your collections.

Secretaries' books from organizations, ranging from the Chamber of Commerce and the Rotary Club to the Ladies' Tuesday Afternoon Study Club, can provide an astonishing amount of source material. Let each organization know that you are acquiring files for your historical society and suggest that each turn over its old records to you. When you do acquire a particularly significant group of records, you could make much of it publicly, with newspaper stories and pictures. That will draw attention to your needs and purposes and thereby stimulate other groups to hand over their records to you.

Businesses will be loath to turn over any recent records, but you can talk to them about the correspondence and other material of two or three decades ago or earlier, with the understanding that periodically they will give you another accumulation. The records of both major businesses and minor ones are important to an understanding of your community.

State historical societies and other large repositories have facilities to copy data for you at a nominal price. For volumes so rare that you suspect you will never be able to acquire a copy for yourself, have pages duplicated. On your copy, indicate the exact name of the book, author, publisher, date, and other pertinent bibliographical material, as well as the page numbers.

Recording historical information

In addition to locating and collecting historical information from available sources, there are some data that you must record yourself.

Cemetery inscriptions deserve collecting. Small cemeteries may be abandoned if churches or villages disappear, and their records can be difficult to locate.

If there is an active local genealogy society, perhaps its members have already compiled cemetery records and will share them with you. If not, you can assign a committee from your group to check the headstones and to copy down the information given there: names, birth dates, relationships, death dates, and other data.

Recording cemetery data is an intriguing assignment for volunteer groups like Boy Scouts and Girl Scouts. The more groups and individuals you interest in historical activities, the more support and understanding all of you will have in the community.

Historic sites of all kinds need to be verified and recorded. Try to identify the exact spots where something of importance happened, using all available plats, not only current but historical as well. Check old diaries and journals for landmark indications and interview old-timers.

Use courthouse records (usually in the office of the registrar of deeds) to identify present and past owners of land in which you are interested, so you will know which people or families to interview. The detective work involved in authenticating precise locations is an assignment for patient, painstaking volunteers.

Record place names, particularly those of small communities that have dropped from sight or are dwindling in importance. A good place to start is to study post office records (the registers of appointments of postmasters), available through the National Archives and Records Administration (Washington, D.C. 20408). Duplicates of these records, available at small fees, give astonishing information about early-day communities. Often the chatty reports tell how and why the names were given.

Map-making

Historic map-making is a fascinating project. Secure a map of your area, with highways, rivers, railroads, and other information marked on it. Maps may be available from the state highway department, from the U.S. Geological Survey, or other sources. (A regular highway map is usually cluttered with figures and symbols.) Have it enlarged to about thirty-six inches in width, so that it is big enough to work with. Mount it on a wall, so that various members can work on it; then have them enter sites of historical interest. Make sure that each site is accurately located and marked, that it has been carefully researched, and that all dates and spellings are correct.

The selling of maps can be a profitable venture over the years. Have the map printed on heavy paper and, if possible, in more than one color of ink.

Community projects

There are many ways in which a historical society can work cooperatively with other organizations within the community to mutual advantage. Because these projects involve two separate groups of leaders, with different basic purposes, cooperative ventures require a great deal of planning and flexibility, but the results can be of benefit to all.

Speakers bureau

One of the simplest projects to maintain, once it is established, is a speakers bureau. Within any community there are a myriad of organizations requiring regular programs: civic clubs, such as Rotary, Kiwanis, Optimists, and the like; social and study clubs; professional groups of accountants, secretaries, lawyers; and many others. If there is no list of groups presently in existence, you can compile one from suggestions from your members.

Develop a committed group within your organization of members who can speak easily and well and who have the time and inclination to write speeches on a variety of historical topics—all well-researched and historically accurate, all interestingly presented. Perhaps you could divide the duties, having some personnel devoted to research and others to preparing and delivering speeches based on that material.

In late summer, or whenever the various organizations are planning programs for the new season, send a notice to each indicating that you have program materials available as a service to the group. Also, indicate that your speakers are available to fill in whenever an emergency arises and the clubs need last-minute help.

In the beginning, you will need to compile a great deal of local historical information: the history of the medical profession, for instance; the role of women; social customs and entertainment; the development of music or drama with examples of early-day presentations; basic political history. You may want to prepare speeches on seasonal activities: how children celebrated Halloween a century ago; how athletics were organized; the household jobs a woman did every spring. You can use all of the research at hand for these speeches, with old newspapers providing little nuggets of colorful detail that add human interest.

Keep a voluminous file of all the speeches. Within a year or two you will have enough material to supply any club with a program on nearly any subject. Your speakers bureau will be limited only by the number of people who want to give speeches.

Each speech should be no more than thirty minutes in length. Each time you speak, mention the historical society, so that members of the audience can learn how they may join.

School projects

It is up to you to introduce yourself to local teachers and to tell them of services you may be able to provide them. Most schools have at least some study of the history of the state as part of the social studies curriculum. Faculty members change, and many of them come from other geographic areas and are unaware of facilities in their new community. They often do not know of the existence of a local historical society.

To be of help in schools, you will need to work closely with the teachers. Tell them what material you have in your society, what resources you have available to them. Offer to help them with research

County retired teachers host society reception in appreciation for the contribution historians make to the community.

and to arrange tours. Many teachers welcome outside lecturers in the classroom to talk to the children about local history and how it fits into the context of the general history of the state.

You will be most successful if you understand the operation of schools. Teachers design their curriculum months or years in advance, so your planning must proceed with theirs. In some systems, there is central planning for curricula, so you must work with a coordinator before becoming involved with the classroom teachers.

If you are to serve as a guest lecturer in a classroom, plan your talk carefully with the teacher so that the subject fits into the curriculum. If the instructor already has given general information to the class, for instance, your topic should be specific.

Use human interest stories for illustrations, selecting them according to the age of the audience. Always allow time for questions and answers. If you do a good job of speaking, you will arouse the interest of the children, and they will want to know more. Children are rarely as inhibited about asking questions as adults. Make the most of the limited class time because when the bell rings, your audience must go.

For advanced history students in high school, you could present a program on how to do historical research, instructing them in the use of records, newspapers, and all other resources in your collection. A good teaching procedure would be to present an actual historical problem and ask students what kinds of information they would seek and where they would look for it. From there you can go into more sophisticated information about research. Invite the students to your historial library to see for themselves what materials you have available. Encourage teachers to assign papers so that students can put into practice what they have learned about historical research. Some schools have participated in internship programs, allowing credit for advanced students for becoming educated in the operation of a historical society.

Students can become involved in oral history projects. Have the teachers or members of the society teach the students how to interview. Ask each one to get material from the oldest member of their familiy or their neighborhood, interviewing them about specific events in the community. Most students can gain access to a tape recorder. Be sure that the teacher will allow you to keep copies of the resulting records and that the interviewees have given permission for you to use the results.

If you have established good rapport with faculty members and the administration of local schools, there is no need to confine your service to the social studies department. If the English teachers are receptive, you could suggest essay topics for composition classes. Again, the resulting papers should provide substance for your collection.

Senior citizens' projects

Senior citizens are often most interested in local history. Many times you will need to take history to them.

Your society can organize gatherings and parties for them. For instance, you could have a storytelling contest about particular celebrations, storms, or specific events. Tape record the stories and do your best to keep the yarn spinners on the subject. Although the stories will have to be verified and edited later on, you will have renewed an interest in history that could pay dividends when you interview the senior citizens individually.

You can ask them about games they played as children on the school playground, for instance, and have them dictate the rules and purposes of the games. Old-timers in groups can spark each other's memories: several people recollecting together can revive more social history than if it were sought individually.

Souvenir books and brochures for annual events give the society an excellent outlet for sharing historical information about the community.

Fair booths

If your community has an annual county fair or other similar activity, your historical society should consider having a booth or exhibit there. Fairs attract patrons of all ages, and a display can serve as a good means of publicizing your group and its functions.

You should have something big and dramatic enough that people can see your exhibit from a distance and something with small details so that when they walk over to look at it, there is enough of interest to justify their stopping.

Naturally, you will take appropriate precautions to guarantee security. Fasten artifacts to walls or the floor or keep them in closed cases.

Pictures, maps, and old newspapers are eye-catchers when they are displayed in an interesting fashion. If you have a number of photographs to be identified, have them mounted so that people can look at them at close range, and have paper available for them to write down what the pictures show and who is in them. You can make the identification of photographs a contest, offering public recognition or a gift membership in the society to the individual who can identify the greatest number of pictures.

Something with action brings attention. You can set up some pieces of kitchen equipment that are operable: a sausage stuffer, a churn, or a frame to cut homemade grease-and-lye soap. You might dress up the volunteers manning the booth in period costume.

You will need to have facilties at your fair booth to enroll new members for your society. Your display must be done well to show that your organization is worth joining and supporting.

Movies

Almost every community has individuals who have taken home movies through the years. Often there are sequences showing parades, civic events, school activities, and even day-to-day pursuits. The public is used to moving images, and old movies are captivating.

With technology changing in the present, no one should be surprised about the problems of dealing with the idiosyncrasies of the past. Sixteen millimeter film was the standard in the early years before the advent of eight millimeter and Super 8. Should you wish to produce a single film for showing, it will be necessary to copy the segments. One alternative is the use of videotapes, if the society has the use of a large enough projection device.

In collecting old film, be very careful of nitrate-base stock, which can be explosive. Convert it immediately to safety film, and do not store it in your facility.

The editing of movies is a time-consuming affair, but a necessary part of your work. It is much easier on videotape.

6

$\blacklozenge$

Oral History

Oral history is the unwritten, unpublished information that heretofore has been only in the minds of individuals. Oral history is what people say about events. It provides colorful, detailed information, usually supplementing other data. In some cases it is the only information available about certain happenings.

In primitive societies with no written language, all of the knowledge and lore of the past was handed down from one generation to the next by recitation of legends. Much of our knowledge of Native American history comes from oral tradition. Stories were memorized by each succeeding generation.

Other cultures, not accustomed to relying on memory, have tended to overlook the "stories of the old men" as historical sources, concentrating instead on written records, journals, and newspaper accounts. Within the past generation, as people use the telephone more and the written letter, diary, or journal less, oral history has become more important to historians. It brings a certain flavor and quality to words and ideas that the written word cannot convey.

How do you get started?

With the development of easy-to-use tape recorders, oral history programs have been established by many historical groups. Many people who intend to write memoirs but never do will talk about what has happened in the past. Getting that information in permanent form through the use of tape recordings is an important historical activity.

To establish an effective oral history program, you need first to identify the people you will interview who are the most knowledgeable sources of information. You need to know how to interview them, what questions to ask, and how to proceed. And you need to know what equipment to use and how to use it.

Within your own historical society, you can establish an oral history committee to make lists of people with specific stories to tell. People to consider might be a farmer who progressed through horse-powered equipment to steam and diesel; a laborer involved in a bitter strike in the key industry in town; a rum-runner, moonshiner, and bootlegger during prohibition; and a mayor involved in key developments in the town.

How do you go about interviewing?

First get in touch with your subject, either by letter or by personal contact, advising him or her that you want to talk about a subject and explaining what your purposes are. Then set up an appointment so that your subject can be sifting through his or her memory, checking through scrapbooks and talking with other people for information on the topic.

While your subject is doing that, you will prepare yourself. You will know in general what questions you will ask: who (get the exact names, not Aunt Sandy, but Alexandra Hones, wife of Marsden), what, when, where, why, and how. In preparation for the interview, check newspaper stories, legal documents, vital statistics, and other material so that you will know what kind of information you do not have but hope to get. If you are unfamiliar with the nomenclature of the particular subject, study the terms the person is likely to use. Try to have someone familiar with the topic do the interview.

Prepare a general outline, referring to it from time to time so that you will not stray too far from your purpose. In many cases, you will not have much of an idea when you start about what kind of information you will find. It is sometimes easy, especially if you are a beginning interviewer, to become so absorbed in the interview that you lose sight of your intent. As you become more experienced, you will rely less on notes.

Arrive on time for your interview, plug in your equipment, and exchange a few pleasantries before you begin. Leave enough space on the tape so that you can later go back and add in the identification: name of interviewer, name of subject, date and place of the interview, and the general topic. If you put all that in at the time of the interview, the subject may be overcome with "mike fright." Many older people are skittish about microphones.

Begin asking questions, phrasing them in terms that will evoke memories. For instance, rather than asking, "When was that?" in your interview, ask, "Was it in the middle of the summer? Before or after the Fourth of July?" Or if your subject was a farmer, ask, "Was it before the wheat harvest?" Answers to these questions pinpoint the exact time far better than if you have asked what month and day the event occurred, and they are more likely to lead to further connections.

For locations, try to get a legal description of the site. In town, get the street names and distance from an intersection. In a rural area, get the name of the township. If the exact location is vital, take a map of the area and have your subject mark it, making a statement on the tape to that effect.

Have a note pad with you. You will want to check the spelling of names, places, and events later.

If there are discrepancies between what the interviewee says and what you feel is the truth, do not belabor the case. Try to get an explanation, but do not antagonize your subject.

Phrase your questions so that they cannot be answered by a simple yes or no, but will require explanations. If your subject seems reluctant to discuss something you really want to know about, rephrase the question. A good reporter, which is what you are, learns to approach topics from different angles.

Avoid interviewing more than one person at a time. You can accomplish far more on a one-to-one basis, asking and answering questions with no outside interference. Spouses are often liabilities during an interview; the one not being interviewed sometimes disagrees about specifics or the relevance of a particular comment. If you wish to interview both spouses, do so separately. You can use the information in the first interview to spur memory in the second.

Many of your interviews will require more than one session. An hour and a half is the longest you will ever want for a single interview. Make an appoinment for the second session as you leave. In the meantime, your subject will probably remember more details to tell you.

After you completely finish your interview, ask the subject to sign a simple document acknowledging that he or she has given this information willingly for educational and historical purposes. The wording of the form, typed on historical society letter-head, could be: "I hereby give and grant to the Smith County Historical Society as a donation for such scholarly and educational purposes as the Society shall determine, the tape recordings and their contents listed below." The paper will be signed by the narrator and the interviewer and will give the date of the tapes.

Other interviews

For your local historical society, you will also interview people who are prominent in business, political, and community life. Occasionally, they may wish to put restrictions on the use of the material published or made available to the public for a number of years. Such restrictions are a headache; avoid them if you can. If they are necessary to obtain the interview, accept them and honor them. For more consideration of legal problems associated with the material of oral history consult Oral History for the Local Historical Society by Willa K. Baum, published by the American Association for State and Local History.

What kind of equipment do you need?

Find the simplest, most foolproof, you can get. Have a tape recorder that is lightweight, easily portable, and always operable. It should work on both regular electrical current and batteries. Be sure to have fresh batteries in the machine and a couple of spares in your pocket. Bring an extension cord and a socket adapter with you as well.

For most purposes, a small, easily carried cassette recorder will serve you well. A separate microphone works better than one built into the recorder. Do not economize on tapes. Buy top-quality stock for good reproduction of sound with a minimum of surface noise. Save the boxes for storage.

When you set up your equipment, do not place the microphone and the recorder on the same table; you will record distressing noices from the machine itself. Set the microphone near your subject, on a cloth or other sound absorbing device to make sure there is no rattle or echo. The microphone should be in a relatively unobtrusive location to make your subject unaware of it as he or she talks. Once you have your equipment in place, do not fiddle with it except to turn the cassette over at the end of the first side.

If your subject is a little ill at ease at first or curious about the operation of the recorder, you could record some idle chitchat, then replay it to let him see how the machine works. That length of tape you could use later for your lead-in, the part on which you later record the name, date, and topic of the interview.

Transcribing the results

As soon as you can, have your tape recording transcribed by one of your volunteers into a typed manuscript. Although the tape remains the primary document, it is possible that a change in technology will make playback in the future more difficult.

Depending on your subject, you may wish to give him or her a copy of the typescript to correct for factual data. Tell the interviewee not to make a written essay of it, but merely to check names, places, or other specific information. Then make those corrections in your own transcript.

In this age of social history, your oral history program will collect important information available nowhere else. You need a bit of talent and a lot of time.

7

♦

Site-Marking

The permanent marking of historic sites can be one of the most frustrating public functions of a local historical society. As with most of your work, planning is vital.

What do you mark?

Look at your own history with an objective eye, and determine what are the most significant historical events of the area. It does not always follow that the oldest is the most important, although you will probably include some of the "firsts": site of the first house, first church, first school.

Then with a calm, collected committee, you will list the sites in order of priority. All things being equal—but they often are not—you will install a marker at the most significant site first and so on down your priority list.

Where and how do you mark the site?

Having decided what to mark, you must then determine where and how to mark the site and what to have on the legend. Markers are permanent; that is why you install them. Do not make a mistake that will last for eternity.

Once you have decided which site is your first priority, begin studying all available records to make sure you have located the exact spot. Whether or not you place the marker there is not important. If for any reason you cannot place the marker on the exact spot, you will want to know, for example, how many feet east of the sign the site was.

The next order of business is what kind of marker you will install. Aluminum ones provide the greatest opportunity for wording. Most state historical societies can provide some financial assistance with aluminum markers. You may wish in some instances to use granite. Whatever you choose should be durable, able to withstand both the elements and the ravages of vandals.

What do you write?

The writing of legends is difficult because you want to tell a detailed, complete story in a very limited number of words. Work on the legend with earnestness, choosing the most striking information and finding single words that will take the place several. Get suggestions from groups that have experience.

What are the legal considerations?

Presumably before you began tramping over someone's property, you received permission to be there. For the location of the installed marker (whether at or near the actual site), you must secure an easement from the landowner. After all, it is on his land you wish to place something permanent. If you wish the marker to be alongside a highway, you must negotiate with various governmental agencies. If you do not have an attorney among your members, hire one to handle these particular legal matters. The attorney will be able to save you from possible difficulties later on.

Maintenance

Another consideration is the maintenance of the marker. Who will see that the weeds are cut near it? Who will return it to its place if it is knocked askew? Determine the answers to maintenance questions before you begin mixing the concrete.

How do you finance your marker?

If it is one that has appeal to a specific group of people, ask them for contributions earmarked for that project. For instance, if it is a pioneer cemetery, ask surviving members of families buried there if they will help. If it is the site of the first factory in town or a brickyard or forge,

Commemorate dates of significance in connection with marked sites by involving other interested historical organizations.

perhaps the Chamber of Commerce or members of an industrial group will help.

How can you cut some costs?

If an old building in your community is being torn down, sometimes it is possible to salvage granite foundation stones or other material suitable for markers. Where will you store the stones? How will you transport them? Do you have a member with a large warehouse with some extra room? And one who owns a boom?

If you use stones as markers, you can have them cut during the off-season, usually winter. Many stonecutters will work for more reasonable fees when they are not otherwise occupied.

Installing the marker

When it is time to install the marker, you often can secure the volunteer services of Boy Scouts or other youth groups, who can earn merit badges for historical work. They can help dig trenches, put together framing, mix and pour concrete, and trowel it. They can help jimmy the marker to the proper location on the concrete foundation. One or two historians supervising a troop of Boy Scouts can accomplish a great deal when it is time to install a marker.

After the marker is installed, you will hold an elaborate unveiling ceremony with appropriate city and county officials present, with music, and with a speaker giving a brief speech about the importance of the site. You will have a gala time, and you will have accomplished something lasting.

8

Tours

Tours show history, geography, and cause-and-effect relationships. Tours are picnics—for everybody except those in charge. Tours are a great means of getting many people involved in an easy, effortless study of their own history.

Planning a tour, a smooth running, happy tour, takes about a year of thoughtful, careful attention to details, historical and otherwise. A well-run tour is a delight; a sloppy one, a fiasco. The difference lies in the planning.

Put the tour in buses, rather than in automobile caravans. If you have a long string of cars, one in the middle always seems to get lost, with the result that the ones following it are lost, too. There are problems of parking, problems of dust, if it is a tour along byroads. Passengers in automobiles cannot have the advantage of hearing the tour guide, and they have no idea why they have come to a site. Also, they miss the camaraderie of the bus ride itself.

Area tours by chartered buses

As soon as you decide what area you want to cover on your tour, get a large-scale map, preferably one that shows all roads. Divide the area into townships, or similar small subdivisions, and assign members of the tour committee to find out all they can about them, one person to a subdivision. If you can have natives, or residents, working on their own area, they will have the advantage of much knowledge already. Each committee member should write down all the possible stopping points in the area and as much general historical knowledge of each point as possible.

With the map of the whole area at hand, plot a possible itinerary, using as little backtracking and zigzagging as possible. Work out your itinerary on paper first.

After you have a reasonably good idea of where you will go, begin research for specific information about the sites: why was this place important, what happened here, to whom, and when? What has happened to the place or the people since?

Even after you have the historical part of the itinerary settled, you have other matters to consider. Where will you have rest stops, with adequate toilet facilities available? (Plan on a toilet stop every two hours.) Which sites along the way will you merely look at from the bus, and which will be get-out-and-look stops? Every time you unload many people from a bus, you slow up a tour; make sure each stop is worth the time it takes. You should arrange your tour so that you have those stops every thirty to forty-five minutes, at particularly scenic spots.

Many of your tour participants will be photographers, amateur or otherwise. When you are planning your itinerary, have a camera buff along to help pick out the photogenic areas or other spots to which photographers will be especially attracted, and allow time in your schedule for camera stops. The photographers on the tour will be unhappy if they are not permitted to get off the bus. They might insist, and unscheduled stops will upset your overall plan unless you have made allowances.

Consider, too, the time of year. Tours along a stream or in a wooded area are often most effective in the fall. Tours in orchard country are prettiest in spring when the trees are in blossom. Weather, too, is important. Do not schedule tours at times when you are reasonably sure the weather will be damp and unpleasant.

One beauty of tours is that they are usually on intriguing little back roads that most people seldom see or even know about. Often tour participants include some people who ordinarily do not care at all about history, but who enjoy the ride and then find themselves involved in history in spite of themselves.

If it is an all day tour—that means a maximum of seven hours, no more—make arrangements for lunches. You can have box lunches provided by a caterer, or you can have each tour participant bring his or her own sack lunch. Arrange a picnic-type stop at noontime at an attractive spot, and be sure restroom facilities are available and adequate.

You will also need a bad weather lunch alternative, just in case: a village hall, a country barn, or some other covered area to protect you from a pounding rainstorm. Make those arrangements in advance so that you are not caught short.

Try to find buses with public address systems. If you cannot, make arrangements to rent or borrow loudspeakers for each bus on your tour. Your tour guides will need to be heard at the back of the bus over the sound of the motor. Make sure that passengers are insured by the bus company. If not, take out short-term insurance yourself.

School buses are an alternative. Their drivers tend to know the back roads, and the lack of overhead racks and arm rests permits egress from the seats. However, the minimal upholstery and springs might quickly turn one's mind far away from the advantages.

You will need one tour guide per bus. The guide should be one of your members who has prepared a great deal of factual information, as well as human interest stories, about each of the sites along the tour and about the area generally. The guide should not read the material but should be able to deliver it in an easy, informal style, and should be able to answer any questions passengers may ask. Let the tour participants add information, too. Sometimes they are familiar with the area themselves and can relate some historic lore. Without a well-qualified guide, the tour could be just any bus trip; with a guide it is a historical experience.

Tour booklets make a tour memorable. With well-prepared material, tour members can relive the tour every time they read the booklet. Ideally, every tour participant is given a booklet or folder that contains a map of the area with the itinerary marked with a felt-tipped pen, a detailed listing of the itinerary and the historical and geographic points of interest along the way, copies of stories or legends about the sites, and other pertinent material you can supply. However the material is copied, it should be detailed, accurate, and interestingly written.

The tour guide or person responsible on each bus may also want to have a totebag of extra equipment for the comfort of the passengers. If the air outside the bus is cooler than that inside, or if the air is humid so that the windows steam over, have a roll of paper towels to wipe them off. It is useful to have a box of tissues, a tin of aspirin, and Band-Aids.

To determine the cost of a tour, add all of your costs—bus charter, meal costs, printing, tickets, name tags, entrance fees, rentals—and gear the cost of individual tickets to 60 percent capacity of the bus. You will not want to conduct a tour for a number smaller than that, and you want to be sure you recover all of your costs from the tour.

You will take reservations in advance, including the names of the tour participants, so you can label tour booklets and produce name tags. Determine a central location for the tour participants to meet, park their cars, and board the buses. Require payment at the time of

Excursions to local sites should be carefully planned and informative.

reservations to ensure that you will not be left with a half-empty bus.

Tours can be among the most exciting historical activities you sponsor. Use lavish publicity through all possible means to create enthusiasm for them.

Alternatives

In some areas, tours by bus are not practical. For one-site tours, participants gather, using their own means of transportation, to visit a particular area as a group, with guides directing them at the site. This kind of expedition is particularly workable for any place where the area enroute is not especially historic or scenic, the distances are great, or the tour participants would be coming from many different communities. The tour is the inspection of the site itself, not the means of getting there.

It is possible, too, to join forces with other local historical societies or the state historical society for longer tours outside the immediate region. Whether it is a half-day tour or one of several days, the same careful planning and attention to detail are essential for a well-run excursion. An overnight tour requires block-booking of hotel space, arrangements for mass feeding, and usually some sort of brief historical lecture or slide presentation in the evening. You can work with a local travel agent for specific help.

Walking tours, town tours

In many ways, walking tours of historic buildings and homes in the community are more difficult to plan than a long bus tour because participants can become scattered all over, not confined to a manageable group. You will need to spend a great deal of time planning what buildings will be open on the tour, making necessary arrangements with the owners, and then establishing the traffic flow. Keep the tour route consistent, so that people go from one site to another in a sequential pattern, and do not mill around in confusion. Make sure that owners' private possessions are out of the way and that a supervisor is in each room to protect against light-fingered tour participants.

Guides should be situated in each building to tell what it is and why it is significant. Tour booklets are not as important for a walking tour as they are for a bus tour, but they can provide historical information that the participants can enjoy rereading after the tour is over. If there are large groups in a tour, some people might not hear the guides. If they have tour booklets, which they can read later, they will end up with a better knowledge of what they have seen.

In some communities, combinations of walking tours and bus tours have been handled with ease. The walking tour is confined to an area only a few blocks square. The buses are at a designated spot, and they then take passengers to sites at a distance.

9

Establishing a Historical Library

After you have begun to collect historical material, you will need to gather it together in a historical library. You must arrange adequate security for your files of photographs and historical material, and you must arrange to make your material available to researchers who wish to use it, keeping it intact all the while.

The simplest and most economical way to establish a historical library is, of course, to make use of already existing facilities, such as the local public library. You must make sure that your material remains under your supervision at all times and that it is not merged into other collections. Be sure that it is in a completely separate part of the building. Title to it must remain in the name of the historical society. Catalogue entries must reflect historical society ownership. This procedure helps patrons locate the information and, therefore, benefits both the library and the historical society. Those who work in the circulating library should not be allowed independent access to your historical collection unless very firm regulations are established. Only responsible representatives of your own society should be allowed to supervise it. At no time should any of your historical data be removed from the room.

The prime purpose of a circulating library is to get material into circulation, with books and magazines and other materials being checked out and taken from the premises to be read and used elsewhere. The mark of a good circulating library is the amount of its material in use. Historical material is different. It is gathered painstakingly, it is irreplaceable, and it should not be allowed to circulate.

Any library is only as good as its system of cataloguing. Once information is put into file folders and archival boxes, it is lost forever unless

Request permission to set apart a section or room for local history collections at the public library.

you have an efficient system of retrieval. Your bibliographical lists will provide the first step toward historical cataloguing. Your indices of material will be the second step. From then on, you will need to develop an efficient system of cataloguing and filing.

If you plan to establish a historical library, get professional help in the beginning. The state historical society may be able to provide personnel to train your volunteers to establish a system. Other consulting services exist as well. You are looking for someone with historical training, something different from training in library science. The concepts that determine the filing are different, and you should be sure that your processor understands the task.

The volunteers who man your library should be trained carefully before they begin their work, so the same patterns, and systems of cataloguing and filing are used, and there is uniformity. The best means of guaranteeing a single procedural system is to work out a manual of instructions that everyone follows.

10

---◆---

Preservation of Buildings

For many generations, the idea of preserving old buildings was alien to the American philosophy of "newer is better." With the whole country onto which to spread, as townspeople needed bigger buildings for expanding functions, they went out from the center of town, leaving the older structures behind to crumble as they would. In the past hundred years, builders have gone back to those crumbling areas and demolished the buildings to make use of the land, often to construct new glass and metal structures on it.

Why preserve old buildings?

Only in recent decades have communities awakened to the fact that most of their old buildings are gone or in danger, that the structures left represent an old and significant past. In many communities, only the threat of a bulldozer will push a town to the realization that it has a fine historic structure that should be preserved, that the building represents part of the heritage of the community.

A town that has all of its buildings of the same architectural period often has a dull sameness to it. A town that has a mixture, a blend of the old and the new, is a challenging one, obviously looking ahead as well as to its heritage, building for the future on the contributions of past generations.

Almost every community has neglected but structurally sound buildings that are representative of architectural and historic eras. Those structures can become eyesores and victims of the demolition squad. The voice of your local historical society is often the only one that will be raised against such demolition. You must provide leadership for the entire community to understand and appreciate the value of its old buildings.

Preservation is different from restoration

At the outset, we must distinguish between two commonly used terms: preservation and restoration. Preservation is the conservation of a structure, the maintenance of its basic design and building materials. In generally accepted usage, preservation is keeping a building in an "as is" condition. Such an effort could be quite an undertaking, requiring massive supports for decaying walls and foundations or patching weak and damaged roofs. The preservation of old log cabins is a case in point, where architects spray or infuse the wood with chemicals to prevent further deterioration and stabilize its condition. Restoration is another step, the physical changing of a building to return it to an earlier time period. This process will be discussed in the following chapter. Reconstruction involves the rebuilding of a structure partly or wholly destroyed by the ravages of time. The Governor's Palace at Colonial Williamsburg is a well-known example of a careful reconstruction.

In the adaptive preservation of buildings, the emphasis may be on saving the appearance and authenticity of the exterior. The interior of

Adaptive preservation of this log cabin as a welcome center for interstate highway travelers gives the society an opportunity to share the region's history.

the building need not follow the original historic period in decor and furnishings, and it usually does not. It will have the necessary fluorescent lighting, stainless steel and glass, plumbing fixtures, and other appurtenances for the efficient conduct of the present-day business. The old building will be adapted to a new use, and although its interior will be new, its exterior will carry the appearance of the original structure.

A fine old mansion can be used as a funeral home or an elegant restaurant. A railroad station can be turned into a shop or a restaurant or even a neighborhood drive-in bank facility. A church can become an office for a monument company or a school. A country schoolhouse can serve as an art gallery. An entire block of business warehouses can be used for offices, stores, and small shops, perhaps far different from the original purposes of the buildings. Rows of early-day flats can be turned into sophisticated apartments. Old barns can become highly desirable residential quarters.

What can your historical society do?

The first step is to determine what you have in the community and then to decide what is worth saving.

You will have worked with the Chamber of Commerce and with key businesspeople to let them know what you are doing and to generate interest and financial support from them. When they realize that the preservation of old buildings and adaptive reuse in the community can be an asset to the whole town, they may join forces with you. In many cases, preserving buildings and putting them to new use rejuvenates a downtown area that is decaying. In other cases, such work helps save a residential neighborhood that is beginning to deteriorate.

The preservation of buildings is a community effort, and you should realize that your historical society may be merely the catalyst that sets the whole undertaking into motion. Your group will suggest, explain, interpret, stimulate enthusiasm, and provide the moral support, even though the implementation of the job probably will be the responsibility of other groups. No matter who does the actual construction of the job, you ought to cooperate fully and provide all the help you possibly can.

To determine what you have in the community, you will need to call in an expert from the outside to make a survey. He or she will not be swayed by emotion but will be able to study the town objectively: homes, public buildings, factories, stores, railroad stations, bridges, all structures. An expert will be able to see what is underneath the redone store fronts, to point out that under the marbleized glass facades, for instance, there are architectural treasures from the Victorian age.

The expert may charge a great deal in order to study your community to give you the professional judgment you want. How do you locate such an expert? Your state historical society may have lists of architects who are qualified to evaluate historical architecture; a school of architecture may have suggestions; or a large-sized architectural firm may have staff people who are qualified. In some areas of the country, there are architectural concerns that specialize in adapting old structures into new uses. The American Institute of Architects may be able to provide you with lists.

To prepare for the study, your historical society should make lists of old buildings to help your outside expert get started, and it should gather old photographs to show how the buildings looked in years past. It may be that buildings your members have completely overlooked have architectural details of distinction that have been covered up or so altered that you were unaware of them, and that buildings you thought were of no particular significance possess some rare qualities.

The expert may make a "windshield" survey at first, listing properties that he or she considers worth saving, and composing the list in the order of importance. The expert will tell how valuable buildings are from an architectural point of view, as well as from an historical one, and will list areas that might become historic areas.

As soon as you have the report, you will want to make it public. You should see to it that the local newspaper publishes stories about it, with photographs. You can organize walking tours (see chapter 8) so that people can see the buildings as they are now and can learn of their past. You can produce slide presentations for community groups, such as the Lions Club and others, to stimulate community support, and you can use radio and television to help you publicize the report about your town and its treasures. Your community must be aware of what your historical society, and others, hope to do with it and for it.

The next step, after you have had the survey made and had it publicized, is to ensure that the properties suggested for preservation will remain intact until they can be developed. You should consider historic districts, if your state mandates them as protected areas, and listing on the *National Register of Historic Places* either the buildings or the entire districts. The state historic preservation officer at your state historical society can provide the name and address of the state agency with which you will work for the listing and will be able to make suggestions about procedures to follow. It does take time to be placed on the

National Register, but the waiting period can be reduced if you do a very careful report and include all the necessary data. The time and effort are well spent, for the recognition afforded will provide status to the project, showing the public that the building is indeed worthy of being preserved.

The job of preserving old buildings and adapting them to other uses is one that not all historical societies want to undertake by themselves, simply because of the cost. But the encouragement of local historical societies is essential to stimulate others, whether they are business concerns preserving an old blacksmith shop or forge to serve as an art gallery; a manufacturing concern preserving the original factory to serve as its office buildings; a group of businesspeople banding together to provide funds to preserve an old block of sturdy, granite structures in the center of town; or a quasi-governmental agency formed to use city, county, and private funds to preserve a whole area of town.

Your society will provide photographs, sketches or prints, newspaper clippings, and any other information from its archives to help recreate the structure as it was historically, before false fronts and dry rot set in. You will work with artists or architects who are trying to visualize the building as it will look after preservation is achieved.

You will want to provide publicity of all kinds to make sure that everyone knows what is going on and its importance to the community. You will lend your society's name to endorse efforts toward preservation of buildings that in turn preserve the heritage of the town. As outsiders are sometimes heeded with more credence than those who live in town, your society should sponsor appearances of outside experts—historians, urban planners, and architects—to encourage the acceptance of the project. Whatever needs to be done to stimulate public interest in the project, your society should do willingly. If there are zoning requirements or other technical problems to be solved before the building can be adapted to another use, your society will lend assistance.

And further, your society will recognize and honor the efforts of all in the community who foster the preservation of significant old buildings by awarding plaques and other tokens signifying your approval and endorsement of the undertaking. These plaques may be bronze or other metal markers that can be affixed to the building itself, giving public notice that the historical society approves the preservation. They may also include some small legend, saying "This building was the site of the first flour mill in the county, erected in 1819, abandoned in 1912, preserved in 1986." The plaque could also say, "This plaque awarded by the Torrington Historical Society for the preservation of this building as a reminder of our heritage," or some such legend.

Whether the preservation in your community is merely one building—a log cabin to serve as a knit shop—or an entire area, such as Larimer Square in Denver, or Historic Pensacola, or those in York, Maine, or Keokuk, Iowa—the role of your local historical society is essential and significant.

11

Restorations

Restoration is the returning of a historic house or building to its condition in a given period of time, the structure and all its furnishings historically accurate. A restoration requires much research and careful attention to historical detail. The building itself becomes a museum.

If there are distinguished old buildings in your community that your historical society wishes to save, you must consider whether you wish to preserve them as buildings or restore them as museums. Restoration is the bringing back of the building to its original purpose, the furnishings, structure, and even landscaping being a faithful portrayal of the original. Adaptive preservation is the retaining of the structure to use for whatever purpose is economically feasible. The building itself is preserved, but its function can be adapted to uses completely different from its original purpose, and its interior arrangement and furnishings can be far removed from the historical period it represents.

Restoration is obviously more costly than preservation, as well as more time and energy consuming. If you plan to restore a building, you must have a good reason for your action.

Why restore a building?

Perhaps the architectural style is particularly significant. It may be a splendid example of Frank Lloyd Wright's design, or a pre-Revolutionary saltbox home, or a residence especially typical of Victorian architecture, with leaded windows, balconies and turrets, fretwork furbelows, and fancy wood turnings. It may be an illuminating example of ethnic heritage, a Sunday House of the German immigrants in Texas or a Swiss chalet in Ohio. Or it may be an ornate castle-like

71

structure built by a family with new industrial money in the early years of the twentieth century, such as the Bellingrath home in Alabama or Stan Hywet Hall in Ohio.

Perhaps an important person lived there or an important event occurred there. Then the building can be restored as a documentary site, significant historically. The homes of presidents of the United States are examples—Mount Vernon, home of George Washington; Monticello, home of Thomas Jefferson; and the Hermitage, home of Andrew Jackson, being perhaps the best known. They have been restored to reflect the period during which Washington, Jefferson, and Jackson lived there. The boyhood homes of some other presidents have also been restored. Those of Lyndon B. Johnson in Texas and Herbert C. Hoover in Iowa, for instance, reflect the years those presidents were youngsters living there, not the years of their adulthood. Insofar as possible, furniture and artifacts are the original ones used in those homes. Where originals have been impossible to find, the furnishings that have been acquired are of the same general historic period and geographical area. Of course, all additions in the restoration—furniture, lighting, wall coverings, and the like—should be carefully documented through wills, inventories, public records, and other sources.

Your community may have been the home of a significant inventor, industrialist, writer, or some other individual of national importance, and the building where he or she lived or worked may be one that your historical society would like to restore to commemorate his or her contributions to the country. Perhaps an important historical event took place in your town. Such a site could be restored to the period in which the event took place.

Perhaps there are restorations that could be made in your community that would be typical of an era. The Bulfinch homes in Orfort, New Hampshire, illustrate a way of living in the Federal period; the restorations in Natchez, Mississippi, show antebellum living in the South; Mystic Seaport in Connecticut demonstrates New England's maritime past; and Stuhr Museum in Grand Island, Nebraska, shows frontier life a century ago. These restorations make it possible for this and future generations to picture vividly how past generations lived, worked, made their living, and spent their leisure time. Living-history restorations typical of an era include those that show farm life of several generations ago and the Shaker Village or other communal villages in various parts of the country.

Other reasons for restorations could be that the buildings are part of a historic section or neighborhood; these restorations are often contiguous to others that have already been restored or preserved by other agencies. The aim is to keep the charm and flavor of an older section intact, be it a residential area or a waterfront section. Then, too, there are buildings that have great local sentiment and for that reason are sufficiently important for your local historical society to consider restoring them to their original appearance.

You must have a logical reason for wanting to restore a building to its original purpose and appearance before you begin the laborious process of making it into a museum. Its status as an old building is not enough.

Administering a site

Having decided that your historical society does want to undertake the restoration process, you must be aware of the problems and pitfalls that may arise. In early stages of the restoration, you will follow many of the steps suggested in chapter 10 on preservation, particularly in enlisting community support and in getting the building on the National Register of Historic Places. You will need professional help from architects, historians, and specialists in many fields to help you begin the actual process of reconstruction. As mentioned above, consult your state historic preservation officer for advice and lists of restoration architects. But before that, there are other, more mundane problems to consider.

How will you administer such a site? Does an organization already exist that will be in charge of it, a legal entity to control it and assume responsibility for it? Who will make the decisions, supervise the operations, take care of the property? There must be a governing body of some sort to oversee the financing, the day-to-day operations, the planning and policy-making that such a proposition entails.

Where will the money come from for the restoration of the building and, more importantly, for its maintenance and daily operation? This includes not only the rebuilding of the elegant old Italian tile roof, which is a visible, glamorous undertaking, but also the heating and lighting bills, the salary of the curator who is there to supervise and interpret the site, the wages of the gardener to plant the boxwood and keep the lawns mowed, and even the wages of the security staff that protects the site against possible human predators. It is easy to aquire a building. In fact, many historical societies have been offered buildings free of charge. The public has not really understood why societies sometimes do not accept them, being unaware that such buildings can become albatrosses. The expense comes after the building has been signed over to the society.

Who will maintain the building? Can you secure funds from the local government, from continuing grants from foundations, from outright gifts? There is little likelihood you will be able to maintain a restoration simply from admission charges. It takes more money than that to pay the janitor who sweeps and dusts and replaces lightbulbs, the seamstress who repairs the rips in the splitting satin draperies, and the multitudinous day-to-day operational and maintenance costs.

If your local historical society is offered a building for restoration, and if after careful, thoughtful consideration it decides to accept the building, you must organize a governing board for it. You will need businesspeople and administrators, as well as historians, to establish policy, set down rules, and determine the purpose and extent of the restoration.

One of the first considerations for the board will be establishing the period of time for the restoration. If the building is one that commemorates a particular individual—the home of Willa Cather, for instance—then determine what particular era you wish for the restoration. Will it be of her early days in the pioneer period of the 1870s, for instance, or will it be of a later period in her life, during the 1920s? If the building is an old bank building, will you restore it to the condition it was in when it began in 1900, or when it was robbed in a spectacular cops-and-robbers event in 1935? The older the building, the more purposes it filled in its lifetime, and the more difficult the decision will be as to the exact period for the restoration. But the period must be established by the governing board and must be written down in the minutes of the governing body's proceedings.

The second task of the board will be to have a study made of the property by an architectural historian or other trained specialist, preferably an expert from outside the community. The first survey may be made by a generalist, one who does not specialize in any specific kind of restoration but who will help you with the master plan.

The master plan

The master plan is the key to the whole restoration project. It should include an evaluation of the soundness of the building. Has dry rot set in, are there termites, are the load-bearing beams sound or must they be reinforced with steel, does the mortar need repointing, is the roof sound?

The plan will include a determination of what alterations have been made to the property since the time of its greatest historic interest. Has a new wing or ell been added that will need to be removed? Have the original windows been blocked in or enlarged? All of the changes that have been made in the structure over the years that affect the authenticity of the building will be noted, so that you will know what work will be necessary to return the building to its original design.

The master plan should include a determination of the exact period to which you wish to restore the building. Your governing body will have discussed the matter at some length, but perhaps the architectural historian whom you engage for professional help will be able to suggest some possibilities that had not occurred to you.

The master plan specifically for the site should include such nonhistoric but essential items as parking facilities, visitor traffic-flow pat-

Restoration of any building requires major commitments of time, energy, and funds. Community involvement will foster a sense of pride in local history.

terns, restrooms, office area, and maintenance service area. You must make provision for these services before you can begin to think about the actual restoration of the site. To help you develop the master plan, you will probably need the advice of a number of experts who have had enough experience with other restorations to realize what is involved.

As soon as you have the master plan sketched out, you will need to list priorities. What is the most important job to tackle first? Second? Third? How long will it take you to accomplish each?

Finally, the expert who is helping you with the plans will help you locate special builders and other construction personnel to handle specific details. Not every carpenter can repair the plaster moldings in the ceiling or the patterned tin. You will need to know where to find specialized workers for many of the esoteric details.

With your master plan in hand, the blueprint of what the site will look like when the restoration is complete, and a rough idea of the cost of such a restoration, you should meet with your board to determine how far you will be able to go and how fast you can get there. You will have to plan your goals for the next several years, and plan the fund drives that will be necessary before you can go ahead. In most cases it will take several years before the restoration is as you have planned it!

You need to remember that insofar as the public is concerned, all you are doing is restoring an old building. You should plan to intersperse the essential but unexciting work with other, highly visible, dramatic improvements. A parking lot is necessary, but not particularly stimulating to the public imagination. The locating, cleaning, and installing of old millstones in the sawmill is far more intriguing. You will use all the psychological ploys at your command, making use of as much publicity as possible for the dramatic aspects of your restoration. For your fund drives, you will want to make use of suggestions in chapter 3 on financing and all of the expertise your board of businesspeople and administrators can summon. Your experts will be able to put forth ideas from previous restorations they have completed.

Interpretation of the site

The last step in the restoration process is the interpretation of the site. Why have you restored this building? What does show? Why is it important? As soon as you have enough of the restoration accomplished to begin admitting visitors, you must work out a means of telling the story in an understandable way. The restoration itself is only as significant as its explanation or interpretation. Otherwise, it is still just an old building. Does the building show the life of an important person, the evolution of a particular industry, a way of living in a period of time?

For visitors to appreciate a historic house, they must know why they are seeing what you present. Was every item in each of the rooms present in the building on July 4, 1776? Did each piece belong to Millard Fillmore? Is everything representative of the type of material available to the rich of your area in the mid-nineteenth century? It is vital to communicate that matrix of information from the start.

To interpret a site, you will need to have exhibits set up in a logical pattern, and you will need to have printed brochures to fill in the gaps. The interpretation of the site is its reason for being.

Restorations are fascinating projects for a local historical society, and they can become focal points for enlisting the aid of the entire community. They require detailed, careful historical research to make sure they are accurate. They need precise attention to administrative detail and overall long-range planning. They call for imaginative interpretation so that their purpose is discernible and valid. Restorations call for energy, constant planning, and large sums of money. Before your local historical society undertakes the restoration of an old building that somebody has given you, consider carefully your responsibility for the varied processes necessary for that restoration.

12

✦

Museums

A local museum is usually the outgrowth of individual collections of objects and artifacts, with many others added as the museum program gains momentum. It is relatively easy to start a museum, but operation is complicated and expensive. Consider the costs carefully before you begin.

Questions to consider

Where will your museum be? Will it be in an old preserved building? A former bank, an old store, an unused railroad station, a fine old home, a new building? Have you considered the cost of preservation or renovation?

Will it be accessible to drop-in traffic, in the main part of town? Will parking spaces be available?

How will it be maintained? Who will pay for the costs of utilities, repairs, insurance, and security?

How will it be staffed? Records kept? Exhibits prepared? Labeling done? Preservation and restoration of materials accomplished?

The costs of starting and keeping a museum are so great that you must consider them carefully before you make up your mind, as a local historical society, that you can assume the responsibility for one.

Financing can come from many different sources. For capital construction, you may be able to secure support from the city or the county, from benevolent individuals, and from businesses. There are seldom federal funds available for capital construction.

For maintenance, you may secure a city or county mill-levy. Added funds can come from admission fees, museum shop profits, membership fees, and donations. It will take constant attention to develop sufficient funding.

After you have financing arranged and the building acquired, you begin the job of moving in, of arranging your materials, of attending to the purpose of the museum. What is that purpose? It is to interpret the past through the display of artifacts and to tell the story of what happened by exhibiting objects in context.

Museums tend to be the attics of the community, both in the positive and negative senses of that image. What do you want in yours, what will you accept, and what do you not want? Do you plan to concentrate on specific subjects, specific periods of time, a specific geographic area? You must decide in the beginning what you want, or you will soon look like the site of a garage sale. Many local museums, long organized, are now having to decide what purpose they really serve, and they are weeding out material that was donated to them and accepted in good faith in years past. Deaccessioning material can cause ill feeling among the museum's constituency.

When you accept donations, be very careful of the commitments you make to the donor in terms of use and display. Most museums have adopted a policy of refusing donations that carry conditions. Have proper legal accession forms for donors and the museum representative to sign, acknowledging receipt of items so that descendants cannot challenge the validity of a donation.

Museum displays should be educational experiences. Just as a picture is worth a thousand words, one three-dimensional object appropriately interpreted is worth a thousand pictures.

Each display should teach. It should not be a hodgepodge collection of curiosities and relics, and it certainly need not include every single object the museum possesses. Do not place objects on display because they fit in a space. Just because Mrs. Smith gave you many things, do not feel that you must keep them together in one exhibit unless the exhibit is about Mrs. Smith. Instead, consider what is needed to make the point of the exhibit.

If you have many kitchen articles of a particular period, display them together, and through the use of labels, tell what purpose each item served. As a backdrop for the exhibit, you could use a greatly enlarged photograph of a kitchen of the period to show the range, the table, and the working space, so that the function of the utensils you display is obvious. A kitchen range poker by itself is a mystery unless the viewer knows what it was used for. When it is exhibited in a logical place with other kitchen equipment, it is part of the story.

Design museum exhibits to provide visitors with a learning experience.

If you have many lace fans, consider what you will want them to show. Will you mount an exhibit that will show the various uses of fans, their evolution, their changes, their artistic differences? Will you indicate through them that they were used as cooling equipment, as flirtatious devices, as accessories to women's fashion? Will the display be entirely of fans? Or will you use only one or two of them in a display of women's clothing generally, to indicate their function as part of a larger picture? How will you use the fans to interpret the past?

Before you begin to organize your displays, consider first what their purpose is. Undertake the research you need so that you will know what each object was, its purpose, its date of common usage, and other facts about its background. Finally, it is time to put the exhibit together. If yours is a group depending on volunteers, try to find someone who prepares displays for a local store or is otherwise familiar with merchandising techniques to help you with your exhibits.

Labeling should be done systematically and in a pleasing manner. No matter how small or impoverished your museum is, take the time, energy, and money to have your exhibits properly labeled so that viewers can understand them.

Use cards of standard material and color, and choose standard lettering for your labels. Modern word processors can obviate the need for professionally printed labels in some instances. Whatever method you choose, see that your labels are attractive, clear, and consistent.

The labels themselves should be terse and succinct, so that viewers will read them. One successful method uses print of different sizes. The identification words appear in large print, to attract anyone who is looking at the exhibit. A subtitle, in medium-size print, of a phrase or a sentence is available for visitors seeking the context of the item. A longer paragraph, in smaller print, provides an opportunity for those intrepid students who want more information on a specific object. There might also be a central label for groups of exhibits explaining how they fit together.

You might think of your exhibit plan as an outline. The overall subject of the museum might be the title of the organization. Three or four or more divisions, chronological or thematic, all relate to the title. Each might possess its own label separate from exhibit labels. Each display case is a separate grouping. Finally, within a display area is the individual object. Each item must relate clearly to the more general topic above it.

You must decide at whom your exhibit is aimed. If your audience will be mainly local, perhaps identification of the donors of specific artifacts is necessary. If you have a national audience, most of your visitors have never met your donors and do not care about their names.

Hundreds or thousands of individuals will be viewing your exhibit. It is impossible to stress too much the need for accuracy in spelling and typing.

There are many more matters to consider about a museum as you establish it and get it functioning. You should take proper measures for security, including some sort of burglar detection equipment. When you begin to install your exhibits, be sure they are secured into place and that all parts of the museum are visible to the attendants on duty. Whether your help is volunteer or paid, make sure to inculcate a sense of dedication.

For a more effective museum, you will need detailed knowledge about specialized lighting in exhibits, about conservation, and a variety of other subjects. Books and technical leaflets from the American Association for State and Local History, curatorial advice from a state historical group, a survey from the Museum Assessment Program of the American Association of Museums and the Institute of Museum Services, and all sorts of other services are there to be used.

The American Association of Museums and its regional groups, the

Celebrate the display of important artifacts in innovative ways.

Smithsonian Institution, the National Archives, the American Association for State and Local History, and other groups sponsor workshops and seminars on various specialized subjects to help personnel in local museums. They are an excellent means of learning new techniques and new procedures. They lead to a better assessment of one's accomplishments as compared with those of institutions of similar size.

13

Volunteers

All historical societies depend in large degree on the services of willing, dedicated volunteers to help with their programs. Small historical societies are absolutely dependent upon them.

Your own officers, directors, and members will, of course, administer the bulk of your activities. But there are many other people in the community who will be available and willing to help you, if you know how to find them and use their services.

Even before you issue a call for volunteers, have specific assignments for them to fill. Make lists of work you need to have done: job descriptions. Then make lists of job requirements and preparation necessary to complete the work. Some work is suitable for young people with active, vigorous bodies and not much historical expertise; some for eager young history students; other work is more appropriate for retirees, with time, patience, and detailed knowledge of the community in the past.

Sources of volunteers are many. Boy Scout and Girl Scout groups have merit badge programs for historical service; other youth groups are also useful. Service clubs, such as Rotary, Kiwanis, Optimists, and others, can supply personnel, as can women's clubs of various kinds. Retirement programs, such as Retired Senior Volunteer Program (RSVP), committees on aging, or senior citizen communities, are also good sources of volunteers. In addition, persons who are not members of any organized group are often interested in history and have the time and inclination to help with historical societies.

Before you begin your own program using volunteer services, you may wish to ask a few people to help you on an experimental basis, to see how you will use their services. Most organizations that rely on

Establish annual programs that feature special recognition for volunteer workers and staff.

volunteer helpers have discovered that their programs work better if every person has a schedule and is on duty at a given time each week.

Having found a working arrangement, you may want to organize your volunteers into a group with a name—Friends of the Museum, for

Honoring media and elected officials for service to the society will encourage their future cooperation.

example—and find a bookkeeper who keeps track of hours. Even in volunteer service, the competitive spirit prevails, and some people will work far more than they otherwise would to make sure their names are at the top of the list of volunteer hours. Once a year, you should have a ceremony to confer pins or some other sort of recognition on the volunteers who have contributed a given number of hours of service to the historical society during the past twelve months. This is your way of saying thank you for their help. In the process, the ceremony draws attention to your work and fosters goodwill in the community.

What are the specific jobs for volunteers? There are as many as there are jobs. You will need many volunteer typists to help transcribe tape recordings of interviews, to type index cards for your library, to type forms, and to handle other office details. You will need volunteers to serve as guides if you have a museum, or as librarians if you have a library. You can use volunteers to help identify pictures, to index newspaper clippings and documents, to research historical sites, to do whatever needs to be done.

Volunteers should never be considered people to do merely busy work and menial tasks. They should be assigned real responsibilities, using their abilities to the utmost. The issue ought not to be whether they are volunteers or paid employees. The society should organize its work so that each person receives proper supervision, so that the work each person does is useful to the organization.

The best programs challenge volunteers with responsibility and require much staff work to make them successful. When your volunteers arrive on duty, have specific jobs assigned to them, with someone in charge to whom they may address questions. Someone needs to be present to supervise their work to make the most effective use of their time and talents. Let them develop within their own abilities. They will be the backbone of your organization.

Volunteers will be far more effective if they know about your whole organization. Periodically, you should conduct orientation meetings to acquaint people who will concentrate in one department with the rest of the operation. The librarians should know about the museum, and the bookkeepers will be more effective if they understand artifact cataloguing. Of course, you should also develop detailed training courses for them in specific areas.

If yours is a historical society with a professional staff, and if there is a college or university in your area, it may be possible for you to work out an internship program with the college, in which competent history majors can work with your professional staff, as unpaid (or, in some cases, paid) assistants, in return for college credit. The college is getting a professional instructor for a few students. The historical society is getting trainable services, and the students are getting on-the-job training in professional historical work, with college credit to boot. The internship program must be carefully supervised by the college history department, to ensure professionalism on all sides. In most cases, internships have been of great benefit to all. Work-study programs using student help are relatively inexpensive, if your society can come up with the necessary funds to match salary payments from a college or governmental agency.

From the ranks of volunteers will come new members for your board of directors, new members for your society, and new enthusiasm for your entire undertaking in the community. Your volunteer program supplies the help you need in carrying out your projects, and it also helps publicize your work generally.

You might also investigate the possibility of volunteers from local companies to help with construction work, wiring, and plumbing. With shorter working hours, longer vacation periods, and earlier retirement years, many people in a community are looking for challenging, stimulating ways to invest leisure time. They are looking for your historical society.

Publishing

The spoken word dissipates into the air; the written word remains. Whether your publishing is merely typing and preserving well-written, accurately documented manuscripts of activities of the past or is a full-scale publishing program, you should consider that the writing of history is an important part of your activity.

The printed word must be accurate

Anything that is published—put into print—will assume great importance historically. "It's in print, so it must be right," is a common assumption. Be sure that everything you write is accurate: names, dates, relationships, names of activities, everything. Document it, if not in the printed version, at least in your files, so that in years to come you can recheck the source.

Much of the support for many local historical societies comes from people who have grown up in the community and moved away, but who have a nostalgic feeling for their hometowns. They especially appreciate whatever historical material is published, for it is really all that they get for their membership dues.

On the other hand, many newcomers in the community want to know something of the background of the town where they live. They also are interested in published material.

Your historical writing and publishing may be on a regular basis—quarterly magazines, annuals, monthlies—or may be a once-in-a-lifetime detailed book, or both. Whatever it is, be sure it is accurate.

If your historical society does not have funds to do publishing itself, perhaps it could make arrangements with the local newspaper to print stories of a historical nature at regular intervals. You could supply suggestions for topics and conduct the basic research, if necessary. If the stories come from your own organization, you will have more assurance that they are accurate than if a staff reporter, particularly one unfamiliar with local history, writes them. Sometimes, however, you will discover that reporters who are long-time residents in the community may be far more knowledgeable about local history than some of your own members. If you take the time to establish good rapport with your local newspaper, you will discover that the staff will be happy to cooperate with the historical society.

Periodicals

If you have the manpower and the financing for a publication that appears on a regular schedule, you will discover that your historical society has something to offer its members, both locally and at a distance, that will stimulate interest in your entire program.

The stories in your publications can be more detailed than those you would publish in an overall history. They can be on less academic subjects, but ones that are important nonetheless.

The research and writing should be carefully done. Each story should be well documented and accurate, although it should be written in an easy-to-read style, not a dry, pedantic one. History can be fun, and you can make it so in your periodical.

The subject matter should be thought-provoking and specific. Rather than a story on "How Our Forefathers Lived," have stories on "Christmas in the 1880s," or "When Crystal Set Radios Were in Vogue," or "When Polio Struck Arthur County." Try to vary the topics to appeal to a wide public and have them represent different periods of history. Stories that your members can relate to, of matters they remember from their own past or have heard about from their parents, attract much interest. For one issue, for instance, you could have a story about dinner parties in your community during the Victorian era, including menus and descriptions of table settings, and for another one, a story about how the town fared during the flu epidemic after World War I. Both are historical, yet each represents an entirely different subject and period of time. Events like the depression of the 1930s are good topics since they are now historical and many of your readers can remember specific details from their own lives. The subject matter is unlimited.

For source material, use newspapers, books, scrapbooks, interviews, legal records, deathbooks in the City Hall, and anything else you can find. One historical society sends a letter to the editor of the local newspaper from time to time telling what subject it is investigating, with an appeal to the public for information and pictures. This use of publicity brings forth specific historical material and stimulates great interest in the forthcoming issues of the periodical.

Historical societies that have museum programs can often correlate the stories in their periodicals with existing exhibits or those in preparation, to serve both as a catalogue and as a historical essay.

The size, format, and frequency of publication vary with the financial ability of the organization, the purpose of the publication, and the ability and availability of time of the staff. Some local historical societies, such as in San Diego, publish magazine-size quarterlies, using color illustrations. Others, such as the Greenbrier, West Virginia, Historical Society, publish once a year. Some have mimeographed booklets.

The editor should be well trained and knowledgeable in English grammar and composition as well as in history. If you must rely on a volunteer for editing, consider a newspaper reporter, an English or history teacher, or someone else in the community who writes well and is interested in historical details. As your publication gains momentum, contributors will be eager to submit their work. All of the material should be factual, well reasoned, and written in a simple, readable, easy style. The editor should reserve the right to make any necessary corrections in the manuscript for clarity and to reject manuscripts that do not meet the standards of the publication. In lieu of payment, your contributors will have bylines on their stories.

When it is time to begin technical work on the publication, work closely with your printer. Ask for suggestions about the most efficient printing procedures. He will know the page sizes that will be the most practical for the press and for paper trimming, the type size that will be the most readable, and other details that will help you have well-designed, professional-looking publications for the least amount of money. You should not choose your printer solely on the basis of the cheapest bid. There are other considerations that may make that choice of printer penny wise and dollar foolish.

Modern printing techniques make the use of pictures economically feasible, and good pictorial content adds much to a story. Be sure that every picture is identified so that your readers will know what it is about, and give credit for the source.

If your publication is on newsprint or unbound, you may wish to consider reprints every few years in book form. If you decide this before you publish your first issue, taking into consideration the size of the book as well as the size of the periodical, the printer can save the negatives for future use. One historical society, which publishes a monthly paper, issues a book of reprints every three years and enjoys income from their sale. Many of those who buy the books are people who enjoyed the original stories and are pleased to have them in bound form. If your publication is a more or less standard size, you may wish to consider offering hardbound copies every three or four years, collecting together enough to make a significant volume.

If you have a continuous publishing program, you will want to consider an index to be published at regular intervals, every year, every five years, or whatever seems to be a workable period. See the section below for indexing procedures.

Books

A comprehensive history of your community is a large project that requires tremendous organization, considerable financing, and huge quantities of hard work. Before you consider plunging into such an endeavor, be sure you realize all of the work and attention to detail that preparing such a volume entails.

Start with its organization. Will you organize it topically, with one chapter dealing with governmental development, another on education, another on business and industry, another on churches? Will you show a cause-and-effect relationship, or merely recount what happened with no attempt at interpretation?

Whatever organizational framework you choose, arrange your book so that it has unity and sequence. Many local histories in the past have been hodgepodge compilations of individual stories, one having no relationship to the next. Those volumes do have some historical value, to be sure, but they could provide much more if they had been organized in an orderly fashion.

You will need a general editor or writer, who will have final authority, and many volunteers to help with research, documenting everything they submit. Assign one group to churches, for instance, and another group to schools, and a third to businesses. Allow each one enough time to collect material, but give a definite deadline so that they will not dawdle. Tell them that their job is to make an exhaustive search for all possible material. It is far better to have too much information than not enough. Eventually you will add all of the source material to your permanent files.

Go to the original sources whenever possible, rather than relying on previously written books. You do not want to perpetuate the old mistakes of earlier authors who have made errors in dates or spelling or facts. One local history author discovered that a book written in 1916, previously assumed to be the historical authority of the area, contained large quantities of material from a volume published in 1890, which in turn copied from a book of 1882. In checking courthouse records, city hall records, and other original sources, she discovered that the author of the 1882 book had miscopied legal records in some cases, exaggerated stories in others, and had made monumental mistakes that had been carried on for years.

If you have a topical organization for the book, with separate chapters on various institutions, work out form letters that you can copy and send out to establishments asking for specific information: name, date of organization, founding members, location of original and subsequent buildings, original purpose and any changes therefrom, and all of the other information you think you will need. Set a deadline for the return of those forms. Ask also for copies of any booklets, pamplets, and other material they may have in their files. Ask for annual reports, financial statements, minute books, school annuals, and any other records that are available.

While the individual researchers are gathering together all of the specific detailed information, the person who is to be the writer, who is in charge of the volume overall, should be reading early editions of the local newspapers. Even if your history is not arranged in chronological manner, you should have an idea of the sequence of events. One newspaper by itself does not mean much, but when you study the newspapers sequentially for a ten year span or even five years, you can discover changes in attitudes, in patterns of living, and other subtle developments that do not show up in any other form. You will also make notations of outside influences that affected the town—World War I, stock market debacles, the advent of television—any happenings outside the community that had a direct bearing on the area. You will make only passing references to those, but they are a frame of reference to explain to readers why certain occurrences took place.

Your volunteers, whether they are the same people who are doing basic research or a separate crew will also collect pictures. The volunteers should be sure to have the pictures identified carefully at the time they pick them up, noting whether they are to be returned and to whom. Make sure the donors understand that it may be several months before the photographs are returned. When you do return them, assign the job of taking them back to the volunteers or others who borrowed them. (Ideally, you would have copies made of those pictures for your own files. Practically, it often turns out that you do not have enough money for that purpose.) Indicate in your captions the source of each picture—"Photograph courtesy of the Pilgrim Society"—so that if you need to borrow it again, you know where it came from. The acknowledgment will also please the donor and will give him or her a feeling of having shared in preparing the volume. Borrowed pictures are a trust, which should be honored diligently.

Pulling all of the information together and writing it is a one-person job. If some of your researchers have the ability and the desire to write the material they have gathered, let them. They are familiar with it and can probably do a better job of interpreting it than anyone else could. But reserve the right to edit, so that those sections are in the same general style as the rest of the book. The actual writing should be done in a straightforward, factual style, so unobtrusive that the reader is not aware of it.

Sources

In preparing your publication, you will use all of the information you have already collected in your library. You will discover where the gaps are. In fact, you may be horrified to find out how little you have, really. You will go out to collect more material. Depending on topics, you will use newspapers, legal records, minute books, school and church records, interviews, and all other sources available for research.

If you are writing a really comprehensive account of your community, there will be material in other locations that will be of use to you. The state historical society will have material, possibly including pictures, and will be able to suggest other sources.

Various state agencies—health, education, industry, meteorology, and others—may have statistical data and other information they can supply about your community, historically and to the present. If your state has a state archivist, consult him or her about what records are available through the archives. The state historical society can tell you whether the state has one and where the office is located.

Federal agencies are a source of material about your community, through the National Archives and Records Administration in Washington, D.C., or through the regional branches whose addresses are given in Appendix B. These records include United States census records from 1790 on, including decennial censuses and many others; maps, records of federal projects (including dams, wartime projects, WPA activities, and many others); and a wealth of other material. Some of the material is available on microfilm, which you can obtain on interlibrary loan from the regional office.

Federal census data gives decennial population figures, places of origin, ages and educational attainments of the population at a given time, and all manner of other information. The Census Bureau prepares specific censuses as well. In agricultural or industrial areas, they tell of farm holdings, crops, livestock, minerals, kinds and sizes of industries and businesses, and a wide variety of other information. It does take time to find out what is available and how to get it, but official sources can provide a wealth of primary source material.

Business records are good sources of local history. If you are doing research on various businesses and industries in your community, it is easier if you have someone familiar with business procedures do at least the basic research, if not the actual writing. That individual can interpet the annual reports, bookkeeping records, and other business data more easily than someone who is not familiar with such procedures. If there are inventions that have contributed to the changing fortunes of the businesses, be sure to describe them and tell why they were important. If outside influences affected the growth of the business, tell about them. Does that company still manufacture buggy whips, or did it change to radio and television antennas?

Your volunteers will also go over local newspapers to make notations of stories about the specific topics they are researching. They will pay attention to legal advertisements as well as news stories and display advertisements. If your state historical society has microfilmed copies of local newspapers, inquire about the possibility of buying copies of the films for your own use. You will then need an inexpensive microfilm reader. If you can rent or lease a microfilm reader/printer, you will find it saves hours of research time by making it possible to have exact copies of newspaper material.

Other sources of information abound. You are limited only by the time and energy of your researchers. For accounts of local musical and theatrical presentations, of commencement activities, of many community undertakings, scrapbooks are great sources of information, particularly if the compilers dated the entries when they pasted in the programs. Even ticket stubs can provide information. One local historical society writing about a Ku Klux Klan chapter had no idea where the general meetings were held, for newspaper accounts were sparse and few other records were available, but a ticket stub in an old scrapbook provided that information!

Footnotes

What do you do about footnotes? You want your book to appeal to the public in the community, and ordinary people are often turned off at the site of little numbers and little type at the bottom of each page; it looks like a textbook. But you also want your book to be a valid historical reference book, with each of the sources adequately marked. How do you reconcile these different needs?

As you are writing the text, you can subtly insert some source information by saying, for instance, "According to the *Old Colony Memorial* of July 20, 1852. . . ." But that is not enough. At the end of the chapter, or at the end of the book, have a separate section for notes. Instead of having the footnote figures in the text, indicate the page number, line, and item, if necessary, to which you refer: "page 56, line 4, data from Table VII, page 352, Seventh Census Reports on Population, United States Department of Commerce, 1870." Any other material you would ordinarily put in footnotes you will include here, too. Serious scholars will bless you, and the nonstudent readers will never notice the section at all.

You will, of course, recognize lavishly the work of all of your volunteer researchers, through an acknowledgment of all of them by name at the beginning of the book and also in your section of footnotes, indicating, for example, that David Buckman did the research for this page or chapter.

Whatever you publish must be accurate, for your book will be the source of local history for generations to come. If you have two or three versions of one event, for instance, you will have to assess which is most likely one—or, in some cases, make reference to all of them. You must decide for yourself how to handle controversial subjects, remembering that the sin of omission is as wicked as the sin of commission. Your crew will need tact, finesse, brass—and endurance.

Even if your book is not meant to compete for an academic prize with professors of the local university, you should try to understand how scholarly writing affects the publication of any local history by a historical society. You are presenting social history, and you should take into account the reality of the conflicts in your town events. In most towns there were both Democrats and Republicans, but unfortunately that distinction rarely appears in local histories. There were even rich and poor. Northsiders sometimes did not like people on the south side of the tracks. Workers occasionally went on strike. Your city is part of the nation, so elements of national history, as they affected your locality, should appear in your book. Local history has its own dynamics and its own format, but you should not forget how it relates to the national history you learned in school.

Choosing a printer

Your choice of printer for the local history book is important, for the job is a big one and the book you produce will be the definitive history of your community for a long period of time. In most cases, it will be fifty or even a hundred years between publication of local history volumes. You will want to have a book that will be worthy of your efforts graphically. Do not scrimp in the printing of your book.

If there is no printer available locally to handle the job—and book printing is a special art—make inquiries from the state historical society and other organizations that have had recent publishing experience. Ask them who they have used for printing and for their recommendations; it is also important to find out who they do not recommend! Ask about the quality of work the printers turn out, their reliability, and their adherence to deadlines. One local historical society discovered midway through the production of its book that the printer, a student-operated shop that was part of a technical college, was going out of business. The society had to scurry around to find someone else to finish the job, causing a delay of almost a year. The resulting book contained two different kinds of typeface, and its overall appearance was not commensurate with the editorial quality. Other groups have experienced unconscionable delays in printing.

Talk to many printers even before you ask for bids from them. See what kind of technical help they will be able to give. Do they have book designers on their staff? Will they make arrangements for binding, or will you need to do that? Will they work willingly with you, taking pride in the project, or will they merely consider this just another job to crank out between others? Before you ask for bids, try to determine which printers will be the most compatible with you. Look at samples of other books they have printed, and even talk to the people who published those books to see if they were satisfied with the service.

When you get to the point of asking for bids or estimates from printers, make sure that all estimates are based on the same terms and qualifications: cost of typesetting, page makeup, printing, number of copies, size of page and type, paper quality, pictorial content and the screen or quality of pictures, and a clear determination of responsibilities. Do the printer's employees read proof or do you; do they make the dummy layout or do you? Do they arrange for binding—and will it be soft- or hardbound? If it is soft cover, what sort of gluing or stitching, and if it is hardbound, will it have headbands (extra stitching glued in for durability), and what will be the weight of the boards?

If you are obligated by law to accept the lowest bid, be especially sure that the estimate sheets cover every possible contingency. Many low bid jobs are low simply because the estimator is figuring the cheapest quality and not including professional services the customer has every right to expect from a printer.

When you draw up a contract with the printer, be sure all of these items are written in, so that you will not end up with inferior paper quality or some other substitution that will dismay you. Deadlines should be clearly stated, both for the delivery of copy from you and for the delivery of the printed, finished volume. Do not rush through the task of selecting and negotiating with your printer. The job that he or she does will stay on the bookshelf for a long time; you will want to be sure that the work will be something of which you can be proud.

On your part, make sure the manuscript is complete in all details before you turn it in and that it is marked according to the printer's instructions so that there are no ambiguities in your directions. Changes cost money.

Indexing

After the manuscript is at the printer's shop, you must begin one of the most important parts of the book: the index. A historical volume, especially, is no better than its index—it is the reference your readers need to locate the information they want.

The printer sets the manuscript into type, then makes proofs to be read and corrected, and finally puts the type into page form. The pages are arranged in segments called *signatures*, which number eight, sixteen, or thirty-two pages, depending on press and page sizes, with each page numbered as it will be in the book. Ask the printer to make two proofs of each signature, one for you to make a last minute check—to be sure that pictures are turned right side around, that the proper pictures are on each page, and that everything is exactly as you want it in the finished book. Check it over carefully, marking any necessary corrections, initial it, and return it to the printer. The second copy you will use to compile your index.

In this modern age of word processing, there is no substitute for a computer. Decide on a glossary of terms for general subjects and print it out for your attention while you are scanning the book. You probably will want to run through the book once to identify the general subject entries and another time for the specific entries.

If you have time for more than one person to index each signature, you will have a double check on entries for the index; even when the indexes are prepared by professional index compilers, they often are not detailed enough. Librarians, teachers who have had library science courses in cataloguing, and people who have done considerable research and know from experience what general topics they seek, all are likely candidates for volunteer help in preparing your index.

Index the book in as much detail as possible. Try to project yourself into the place of a researcher fifty years from now who is trying to find specific details in your volume. History students will want to know where people's names are, where specific issues are mentioned, where general topics are discussed.

Within the general entries you will give special assistance to readers. For instance, under "Schools," you may want to make "also see" entries, such as "see athletics," or "see music," or "see population," for entries in those classifications that have relevance to the general subject of schools. The more detail you have in your index, the more useful the index is. Rather than merely saying "Irrigation, p. 283," it is better to say "Irrigation, public meeting about legal problems, 1967, p. 283."

Indexing is sometimes tedious, but it is essential to any volume on local history. Allow plenty of time for it.

Financing periodicals

In the case of regular periodicals, publishing costs can and should come from your regular budget, with your membership fees covering the subscription price. You might also go to local businesses with the suggestion that they support the printing costs of individual editions. Display their names and the notice of their gifts prominently near the masthead, and mention their gift in other publicity. For a monthly, if you can find twelve donors annually, you can save the society a lot of out-of-pocket expenses, without a great deal of burden to a single donor.

You will also need to apply at the post office for a postal permit for a nonprofit organization, bulk rate for mailing, or a second class mailing permit, which also has a special nonprofit category. The bulk rate permit can also be used for other mailings of the society. Although you have to presort the mail, the cost is a small percentage of first-class postage.

Financing books

For a detailed historical volume, you certainly will need financing beyond your own treasury. This can come from grants from the city or county government, Chamber of Commerce help, or local business support—banks, local businesses and industries, alumni funds, or pre-publication sales. Another possibility is seeking special donations from members or friends especially for the book.

How do you figure the selling price of a book so that you can take orders before publication? First of all, you need to know how many copies of the book to have printed, and then figure the cost per book, based on the total printing bill, advertising costs, and whatever else you will spend in production and promotion. Price each book at least five times its actual cost in order to leave room for wholesaling and retailing.

You are likely to be the publisher, who will promote the book to outlets (even if you are one of the outlets). The outlets will have to pay you an amount that will allow you to recover the cost of printing even if you do not sell all of the books. The sales outlets will have to mark up the book to make a profit before selling it to the public. The outlets will have enough margin in order to allow for discounts to members or for promotional sales. Thus, a book that cost $5 to print might have to bring $25 from the public.

While it is true that frequently you will serve different groups, be certain that there is profit for each of them on the sale of a book. You will be most successful if your distribution network is wide. While it is true that your members will be the best audience, they will not be the only audience. You will need bookstores, historical societies, and other organizations to sell the books to their members. It is not reasonable to ask any outlets to distribute the book without profit.

The determination of how many copies to have printed is partly scientific but largely guesswork. As a rule of thumb, you should figure on having the books available for sale over a twenty-year period. Local county histories are not best-sellers. They have their greatest burst of sales in the first year or two after they are published. But because of their nature, they do have continuous sales—smaller ones, to be sure—over a long period of time, as genealogists, grandchildren of old-timers, history buffs, and newcomers hear about them. Some overly conservative editors figure too short and have to order reprints of their books in a year or two, a procedure more costly than if they had ordered a sufficient number when the books were on the press. Overly enthusiastic souls order an unrealistically high number, more than they could sell in a century. Consider how many people live in the community, what percentage of families—not individuals—would be interested in buying the book, and how many you will be able to sell to old-timers now living elsewhere. Possibly half your sales will come from outside the immediate area, from people nostalgic about the Old Home Town.

Some local historical societies make a concentrated sales effort before the book goes to the printer. From prepublication sales, they make enough money to pay almost the entire cost. Do not count on being able to do that; most groups must rely on outside help to underwrite the publication costs. In a few unfortunate situations, the editor or writer has signed a note to cover the printing costs in hope of getting the money back from sales. This procedure is not recommended.

Only as a last resort should you consider selling and printing advertisements from local concerns. With advertisements, the volume appears to be not so much of a history book as an extension of the high school annual or publicity brochure. If it seems that this means is the only way to raise enough money to print a local history, be sure to have an Internal Revenue Service ruling about that revenue before you begin.

Merchandising periodicals

For your periodicals, get alumni lists from the local schools and send well-written letters to out-of-town graduates, playing on nostalgia, telling them about your publication. Be sure the application blank lists the membership price, with a note on how to join the society. Get lists of newcomers from the Chamber of Commerce, real estate agents, Welcome Wagon, or utility meter deposit lists, and send letters to them.

See that every organization in town has a copy to show at meetings so that members can see it and will know how to join the society. Have a copy at the local library for people to see. Have copies at all school libraries.

Have copies of your periodical and subscription forms wherever

Using a society meeting or special community reception to display original material from your publications is an effective way to publicize and market new books or gain periodical subscriptions.

people are—grocery stores, filling stations, department stores, bulletin boards—so that people can see them and can subscribe easily. Have your publications available at your own sales desk, of course, and at all tourist stops in the area—motel gift shops, highway cafes, service stations. Tourists often will buy books or pamphlets faster than townspeople will, simply to know about the area they are in now.

Merchandising books

For your detailed history book, you will need even more specific merchandising techniques. Have leaflets printed describing your book—how big it is, what it covers, how many pictures it has—and distribute them in the same places mentioned for periodicals. Tell where it can be bought and for how much. Have coupons available. People will fill in coupons faster than they will write a note.

Send review copies to book editors of the newspaper in your area and send a review copy to the state historical society suggesting it review the book in its publication. If you think the book is of unusual significance historically, send review copies to other historical organizations that publish.

Prepare a printed brochure, even though it will cost money, and mail copies to schools, libraries, and colleges in the area. Also, send those flyers to people on your alumni lists.

Try to gear your publication date for Christmas sales or for a time when the community is having some sort of anniversary celebration that will draw attention to the past. Have your book new and fresh and sparkling at a time when people will want to buy it.

Use all the facilities at your command to publicize it. Try to arrange a window display in your local bookstore or department store and an autographing party for your author in that store. Talk to history and social studies teachers in the schools to see if there is a way to coordinate efforts. It may be possible from time to time for them to make assignments from the book. Arrange interviews for the author or committee with newspapers, Sunday magazines, radio and television programs. You have spent much effort and money to produce the book. Do not be shy about promoting it. One of the most exciting things on earth is your first look at your newly printed, newly bound book.

Newsletters

Most historical societies will need to publish newsletters from time to time to advise their members about activities and programs. These newsletters are not about history. They are about the historical society. They should be thought of as "what we're up to now" publications, and they should be carefully prepared, both in content and form. They project your society to the public: a sloppy newsletter indicates a careless, less than first-rate historical society.

They also give follow-up stories about completed programs: how much money was raised by the carnival, how many people attended a program, or went on a tour, how many members have now joined. They can include requests for items for a particular museum display, for information about a subject, for suggestions about projects in the future.

Newsletters are the means by which the society and its members keep in touch. The larger the society membership, the greater the need for this means of communication. If yours is a small local historical society with limited means, which also has a regular historical periodical, you can consider using one publication for both purposes, using the same page in every issue for historical society information. The same postal permit requirements apply to newsletters as to other historical periodicals.

Other publishing

Occasionally, your historical society will be involved with other publishing, whether it is brochures about the museum, catalogues of your collections, maps, leaflets, or any of a dozen other projects. By now you will have established a good rapport with a printer, one who has the facilities and the desire to help you plan your printing. You have confidence in him or her and you will keep in close touch, paying attention to details. You have your logo, or identifying mark, which people associate with your historical society, and you use it in varying sizes in all of your publishing endeavors, so that readers automatically associate your society with the publication.

You realize that anything that is printed under your name will project the image of your group to the public. Whatever you publish that is about history is accurate, carefully researched, and carefully documented. Whatever you publish is well written, grammatically correct, and attractive in appearance, with neatness and aesthetic appeal. You do not take shortcuts nor settle for less than the best, for you want the public to know that your historical society is a quality one.

Conclusion
The History Connection

◆───────────

A historical society is a part of two communities. Not only are you serving the geographical area or thematic group that defines your interest, you are also a part of all people who work with history. You must maintain the standards of historical societies, and you must cooperate with scholars interested in your research facilities.

Planning is the key to your success. When you initiate your organization, when you change directions, when you begin new projects, or when you begin your year, you must engage in careful planning. Everything you do will be more efficient if you and your entire group know why you are proceeding.

Most people involved with historical societies get a great deal of satisfaction from their connection with history. The people you meet are fascinating. The work you accomplish is worthwhile. Your effect on the future is notable.

Appendixes

———◆———

APPENDIX A

◆

Suggested State/Provincial Resources

Agencies most likely to answer general questions about historical society activities in each state or province are listed below.

United States

Alabama Department of Archives and History
624 Washington Avenue
Montgomery, Alabama 36130

Alaska Historical Library
Pouch G, State Capitol
Juneau, Alaska 99801

Arizona State Department of Library, Archives, and Public Records
State Capitol, Suite 200
1700 West Washington
Phoenix, Arizona 85007

Arkansas Historical Association
History Department
#12 Ozark Hall
University of Arkansas
Fayetteville, Arkansas 72701

Arkansas History Commission
Parks and Tourism
#1 Capitol Mall
Little Rock, Arkansas 72201

Historical Society of Southern California
200 East Avenue
Los Angeles, California 90031

California State Department of Parks and Recreation
P.O. Box 2390
Sacramento, Caifornia 95811

Conference of California Historical Societies
University of the Pacific
Stockton, California 95211

State Historical Society of Colorado
1300 Broadway
Denver, Colorado 80203

Connecticut League of Historical Societies, Inc.
Killiam's Point
Branford, Connecticut 06405

Historical Society of Delaware
505 Market Street
Wilmington, Delaware 19801

Florida Bureau of Archives and Records Management
Division of Library and Information Services
R. A. Gray Building
500 South Bronough Street
Tallahassee, Florida 32301

Florida Historical Society
University of South Florida Library
Tampa, Florida 33620

Georgia Department of Archives and History
Office of Secretary of State
330 Capitol Avenue; SE
Atlanta, Georgia 30334

Georgia Historical Commission
116 Mitchell Street, SW
Atlanta, Georgia 30303

Bernice Pauahi Bishop Museum
1525 Bernice Street
P.O. Box 19000-A
Honolulu, Hawaii 96817

Idaho State Historical Society
610 North Julia Davis Drive
Boise, Idaho 83702

Illinois State Historical Library
Old State Capitol
Springfield, Illinois 62701

Indiana Historical Bureau
Indiana Library and Historical Department
140 North Senate Avenue
Room 408
Indianapolis, Indiana 46204

Iowa State Department of History and Archives
East 12th Street and Grand Avenue
Des Moines, Iowa 50319

Kansas State Historical Society
Memorial Building
120 West 10th Street
Topeka, Kansas 66612

Kentucky Historical Society
300 West Broadway
Frankfort, Kentucky 40601

Louisiana Historical Society
2727 Prytania Street
New Orleans, Louisiana 70130

Maine Association of Museums
P.O. Box 798
Augusta, Maine 04330

Maryland Historical Society
201 West Monument Street
Baltimore, Maryland 21201

Bay State Historical League
185 Lyman Street
Waltham, Massachusetts 02154

Bureau of History
Michigan Department of State
717 West Allegan Street
Lansing, Michigan 48918

Minnesota Historical Society
690 Cedar Street
St. Paul, Minnesota 55101

Mississippi Historical Society
100 South State Street
P.O. Box 571
Jackson, Mississippi 39201

State Historical Society of Missouri
1020 Lowry Street
Columbia, Missouri 65201

Montana Historical Society
225 North Roberts
Helena, Montana 59620

Nebraska State Historical Society
1500 R Street
P.O. Box 82554
Lincoln, Nebraska 68508

Nevada State Historical Society
1650 North Virginia Street
Reno, Nevada 89503

New Hampshire Historical Society
30 Park Street
Concord, New Hampshire 03301

League of Historical Societies of New Jersey
Green Village Road
P.O. Box 531
Green Village, New Jersey 07935

New Jersey Historical Commission
Department of State
4 North Broad Street, CN-305
Trenton, New Jersey 08625

Museum of New Mexico
113 Lincoln Avenue
P.O. Box 2087
Santa Fe, New Mexico 87504

New York Office of the State Historian
New York State Museum
Empire State Plaza
Albany, New York 12230

North Carolina Division of Archives and History
Department of Cultural Resources
109 East Jones Street
Raleigh, North Carolina 27611

State Historical Society of North Dakota
State Historical Board
North Dakota Heritage Center
Bismarck, North Dakota 58505

Ohio Historical Society
1982 Velma Avenue
Columbus, Ohio 43211

Oklahoma Historical Society
Wiley Post Building
2100 North Lincoln
Oklahoma City, Oklahoma 73105

Oregon Historical Society
1230 S.W. Park Avenue
Portland, Oregon 97205

Pennsylvania Historical and Museum Commission
P.O. Box 1026
Harrisburg, Pennsylvania
17108-1026

Rhode Island Historical Society
110 Benevolent Street
Providence, Rhode Island 02906

South Carolina Department of Archives and History
1430 Senate Street
Columbia, South Carolina 29201

South Dakota State Historical Society
900 Governors Drive
Pierre, South Dakota 57501

Tennessee Historical Commission
701 Broadway
Nashville, Tennessee 37203

Texas Library and Historical Commission
1201 Brazos
Box 12927
Austin, Texas 78701

Texas State Historical Association
2/306 Sid Richardson Hall
University Station
Austin, Texas 78712

Utah State Historical Society
Department of Community and
    Economic Development
300 Rio Grande Street
Salt Lake City, Utah 84101

Vermont Historical Society
Pavilion Building
109 State Street
Montpelier, Vermont 05602

Virginia Historical Society
428 North Boulevard
P.O. Box 7311
Richmond, Virginia 23221

**Eastern Washington State
    Historical Society**
West 2316 1st Avenue
Spokane, Washington 99204

**Washington State Historical
    Society**
315 North Stadium Way
Tacoma, Washington 98403

**West Virginia Department of
    Culture and History**
Archives and History Division
The Cultural Center
Charleston, West Virginia 25305

**State Historical Society of
    Wisconsin**
816 State Street
Madison, Wisconsin 53706

**Wyoming Archives, Museums, and
    Historical Department**
State Office Building
Cheyenne, Wyoming 82002

Canada

Historical Society of Alberta
95 Holmwood Avenue, NW
Station C, Box 4035
Calgary, Alberta T2V 3H3

**British Columbia Provincial
    Museum**
Heritage Court
675 Belleville Street
Victoria, British Columbia
    V8V 1X4

New Brunswick Museum
277 Douglas Avenue
Saint John, New Brunswick
    E2K 1E5

**Royal Nova Scotia Historical
    Society**
Public Archives of Nova Scotia
6016 University Avenue
Halifax, Nova Scotia B3H 1W4

Nova Scotia Museum
1747 Summer Street
Halifax, Nova Scotia B3H 3A6

Canadian Historical Association
Public Archives of Canada
395 Wellington Street
Ottawa, Ontario K1A 0N3

Ontario Historical Society
78 Dunloe Road, Room 207
Toronto, Ontario M5P 2T6

Public Archives of Prince Edward Island
P.O. Box 1000
Charlottetown, Prince Edward
  Island C1A 7M4

L'Institut Canadien de Quebec
37 Rue Sainte-Angele
Quebec, Quebec G1R 4G5

Saskatchewan History and Folklore Society, Inc.
1860 Lorne Street
Regina, Saskatchewan S4P 2L7

Saskatchewan Archives Board
University of Saskatchewan
Library Building
Saskatoon, Saskatchewan
  S7N 0W0

APPENDIX B

---◆---

Regional Branches of the National Archives and Records Administration

The National Archives, Washington, DC 20408, document American history from the First Continental Congress and include the permanently valuable records of the three branches of the Federal Government.

The eleven regional archives branches preserve and make available for research use those United States Government records of permanent value created and maintained by field offices of Federal agencies that are useful primarily for documenting regional and local activities.

Records common to the branch offices include records of District Courts of the United States, records of the United States Courts of Appeals, records of the Bureau of Indian Affairs, records of the Bureau of Customs, records of the Office of the Chief of Engineers, and others, including Bureau of Land Management and National Park Service, Forest Service, and many others.

New England Region
(Serves Connecticut, Maine,
   Massachusetts, New Hampshire,
   Rhode Island, and Vermont.)
380 Trapelo Road
Waltham, Massachusetts 02154

Northeast Region
(Serves New Jersey, New York,
   Puerto Rico, and the Virgin
   Islands.)
Building 22
Military Ocean Terminal
Bayonne, New Jersey 07002

Southeast Region
(Serves Alabama, Georgia, Florida,
   Kentucky, Mississippi, North
   Carolina, South Carolina, and
   Tennessee.)
1557 St. Joseph Avenue
East Point, Georgia 30344

Great Lakes Region
(Serves Illinois, Indiana, Michigan,
   Minnesota, Ohio, and Wisconsin.)
7358 South Pulaski Road
Chicago, Illinois 60629

Mid-Atlantic Region
(Serves Delaware and Pennsylvania;
  for the loan of microfilm also
  serves the District of Columbia,
  Maryland, Virginia, and West
  Virginia.)
9th and Market Streets
Room 1350
Philadelphia, Pennsylvania 19107

Rocky Mountain Region
(Serves Colorado, Montana, North
  Dakota, South Dakota, Utah, and
  Wyoming.)
Building 48, Denver Federal Center,
  P.O. Box 25307
Denver, Colorado 80225

Southwest Region
(Serves Arkansas, Louisiana, New
  Mexico, Oklahoma, and Texas.)
501 West Felix Street
P.O. Box 6216
Fort Worth, Texas 76115

Central Plains Region
(Serves Iowa, Kansas, Missouri, and
  Nebraska.)
2312 East Bannister Road
Kansas City, Missouri 64131

Pacific Sierra Region
(Serves California except southern
  California, Hawaii, Nevada except
  Clark County, and the Pacific
  Ocean area.)
1000 Commodore Drive
San Bruno, California 94066

Pacific Southwest Region
(Serves Arizona; the southern
  California counties of Imperial,
  Inyo, Kern, Los Angeles, Orange,
  Riverside, San Bernardino, San
  Diego, San Luis Obispo, Santa
  Barbara, and Ventura; and Clark
  County, Nevada.)
24000 Avila Road
P.O. Box 6719
Laguna Niguel, California 92677

Pacific Northwest Region
(Serves Alaska, Idaho, Oregon, and
  Washington.)
6125 Sand Point Way, NE
Seattle, Washington 98115

APPENDIX C

◆

Criteria for Evaluation for the National Register of Historic Places

The following statement is taken from the leaflet of the National Register of Historic Places. The leaflet is available from the National Park Service, USDI, Washington, D.C.

The following criteria are designed to guide the states, federal agencies, and the Secretary of the Interior in evaluating potential entries (other than areas of the National Park System and national historic landmarks) for the National Register:

The quality of significance in American history, architecture, archeology, and culture is present in districts, sites, buildings, structures, and objects that possess integrity of location, design, setting, materials, workmanship, feeling, and association, and:

A. that are associated with events that have made a significant contribution to the broad patterns of our history; or

B. that are associated with the lives of persons significant in our past; or

C. that embody the distinctive characteristics of a type, period, or method of construction, or that represent the work of a master, or that possess high artistic values, or that represent a significant and distinguishable entity whose components may lack individual distinction; or

D. that have yielded, or may be likely to yield, information important in prehistory or history.

Ordinarily, cemeteries, birthplaces, or graves of historical figures, properties owned by religious institutions or used for religious purposes, structures that have been moved from their original loca-

119

tions, reconstructed historic buildings, properties primarily commemorative in nature, and properties that have achieved significance within the past 50 years shall not be considered eligible for the National Register. However, such properties will qualify if they are integral parts of districts that do meet the criteria or if they fall within the following categories:

A. a religious property deriving primary significance from architectural or artistic distinction or historical importance; or

B. a building or structure removed from its original location but which is significant primarily for architectural value, or which is the surviving structure most importantly associated with a historic person or event; or

C. a birthplace or grave of a historical figure of outstanding importance if there is no other appropriate site or building directly associated with his productive life; or

D. a cemetery which derives its primary significance from graves of persons of transcendent importance, from age, from distinctive design features, or from association with historic events; or

E. a reconstructed building when accurately executed in a suitable environment and presented in a dignified manner as part of a restoration master plan, and when no other building or structure with the same association has survived; or

F. a property primarily commemorative in intent if design, age, tradition, or symbolic value has invested it with its own historical significance; or

G. a property achieving significance within the past 50 years if it is of exceptional importance.

Index